*OneSelf*

# Have faith. In yourself.

# MARK BRADFORD

Copyright © 2018, 2022 Mark Bradford

Printed in the United States of America
Second Printing, 2022

Alchemy

ISBN: 1-7336622-0-0
ISBN-13: 978-1-7336622-0-8
Library of Congress Control Number: 2019901122

markbradford.org
**v1.5**

# DEDICATION

To those that have faith and those that don't.

To those that are sometimes lost and to those that
are sometimes found.

To those that are members of an organized religion.

To those that are spiritual but not religious.

I dedicate this to you.

Believe it or not, it doesn't matter…

iv

# CONTENTS

# ACKNOWLEDGMENTS

I'd like to thank anyone who has been honest with me regarding their beliefs, and in turn been honest with themselves.

Thank you.

# Introduction

Religion.   As arguably the deepest and most profound of subjects, one must tread lightly. I have no idea how many books are written in modern times that introduce a "new religion."   This is not a book about vibrations or crystals or potions.   This is also not a book about something that happened thousands of years ago or writings that were found on a scroll or a tablet or a cave wall.

This is instead a book about a hypothetical concept —one that if correct is correct *in spite of* or *regardless of* your awareness or belief in it.

I do not mean to, or intend to disparage any beliefs, including yours, or your lack thereof. See *I'm Sorry* at the end of the book if I end up offending you anyway.   My tone in this book is of one who is discussing a subject that is as serious as one can get to some, while being utter fantasy to others. What other subject could possibly have this kind of polarizing affect, and have this variance in meaning to people? For example: if you are into horseback riding, and you tell someone about this, no one ever tells you that "horses don't exist." If you enjoy cooking no one ever says, "Well that's nice but food just isn't for me—I get along just fine without it, please don't discuss it again in mixed company." Nor are there people who go around telling you that you should try their hobby that is invisible, probably costs money, and is going to be a lifelong commitment whether you want it to be or not—and it's a hobby they believe you already have.

It literally means *everything* to some people, and *nothing* to others. There is nothing else in life that carries that infinite ultimate importance to some and has absolutely no value to others. That, in and of itself, speaks volumes of the complexities of this subject.

# This may or may not be a work of fiction—it depends entirely on your perspective.

I'm going to examine and explore religion a bit in the beginning of this book. To that end, I'm going to ask you questions—sometimes naively. They truly are questions in an attempt to understand.

## Religiously

Granted, there are a lot of books that talk about things in a religious *manner* or with a *religion-like commitment* to it. Such books can take any form, really—a book devoted to cycling, fitness, personal improvement, even gardening. "Cycling is my life" tells you that someone cycles *religiously*—they have a commitment and all encompassing desire to be part of this activity. It's more than an activity; it's their life. You get that. If you are devoted to your organized religion then this type of behavior may irritate you, especially if the person expressing it seems to have no actual religion.

But that's not what this book is about. It's not about a religious devotion to a non-religious subject. Instead it is about a concept that may or may not exist—one that just is—and its existence or lack thereof does not have any bearing on whether you should believe it or not.

If that statement feels surprisingly easy to be on board with then what you're about to read is probably going to be pleasant, enlightening, thought-provoking and entertaining. If not, then perhaps you'll read on anyway, and I can clarify.

This may or may not be a work of fiction—it depends entirely on your perspective.

Here comes the part where I offend you.

OneSelf

# *Religion is like a smile on a dog*

Religion can be a very selfish thing. And when you throw it in everyone's face it becomes even more selfish, and the opposite of what it is intended to be.

That's a really strong statement. I don't mean to be harsh, but I am making a point about a concept that is potentially ever-present in one person's life, but completely non-existent in another person's life. Even a vocation is not as ingrained into someone's life the way organized religion can be.

For example, if you are a doctor you may talk about being a doctor at length, make lots of references about what it took to become one, the education, the training, putting in the hours, even the trials of the E.R. However, being a doctor is not really going to change the way you treat your children[1], or affect what you wear, or cause you to quote things and put them all in the context of the fact that you are a doctor. And it is not going to make you assume that I am also a doctor. And if you find out that I am not, it is doubtful you will try to convert me to being a doctor.

On top of all that, you will not ever suggest that I am *already* a doctor but just don't know it.

It's a paradox that the thing that is supposed to make you humble—and not think about yourself—is really making you *not* humble and *is* making you put yourself first. That is the experience many people have when interacting with people who profess to have a strong faith—even those that are a member of the *same* faith. That's not to say it's the only experience they have but it is a reoccurring experience, and I can personally attest to that. Has this ever been your experience?

If you say you are "putting God first" then what are you really saying? What does that mean, in practice? It means you have an action item that is the top of your priority list. And in many cases, admittedly, is a priority that is higher than your job, your spouse, and, even, your children.
But where does this action item live? What are the tasks involved in service to this action item? In

---

[1] Not arguing ability to care for them financially, your presence in their lives due to hours, stress, etc.

6

simple terms, if I am standing next to you, and you put "God first" what do we do now? How does that change our interaction? Do we still get to have coffee or a beer? Does it change who pays for it? Does it change what we talk about?

## The Instruction Book Written By Other People

If you are devout in your religion then you undoubtedly follow The Instruction Book That Was Written A Long Time Ago So You Can't Ask The Author For Clarification, right? The instruction book will tell you how to act, what to do when a thing happens, and even things like what you can and cannot drink, eat, and wear. In addition you are probably instructed by a hierarchy of people who have been assigned roles—each role in the hierarchy is higher than the last—giving it, and them, more and more power over you.

So, you follow the instructions of the book, and the interpretation of the people assigned to interpret it and thus tell you what to do. If you are part of this particular system—a system known as "organized religion" and if you are "putting God first" then you are actually putting the needs wants and desires of the hierarchal system and the participants and leaders first.

Or, more commonly, you may participate peripherally in such a way that you feel you are "doing your part." That part may range from being an "active member" and serving as one of the leaders in the hierarchy all the way down to just attending the gathering now and then, perhaps to sing a song or two and participate in a ceremony.

So what? The point is that none of these things are actually directly *serving* a deity. Where is God in this equation? Where is the worship?

## Serving a Deity

The concept of service to a person, place, thing or deity means that you are doing something to benefit it. And if your service to this thing is placed as a priority above all else including your very own children, then your actions are being donated to something outside of your life—by definition. Yes, you can argue that it *is* part of your life, but let's stay with this simple example.

*"What does God need with a starship?"*

*—Captain Kirk, Star Trek V*

In addition, the concept of service to an entity that is all-powerful and all-knowing is nonsensical at its very simplest core. What is the point of pouring water into a lake that is infinitely large? What is the point of revering a thing because you were *told* to? How does that benefit the entity? It makes sense in

8

the context of fiction, in which an entity controls and manipulates a group of people to gain things it cannot possess itself—thus making it not all-powerful or all-knowing. But, if you were to create a race of sentient beings that could essentially do anything with their lives, would you have any interest in making them spend a portion of it telling you how wonderful you were? Would that not be a waste of their time and energy in these lives that had near infinite options and opportunity? Would you want them to spread the word? To what end? Wouldn't you want the opposite—to step out of the way to see just what they would do—good or bad?

If you must insist on some sort of instruction booklet, wouldn't you leave out any parts that cause them to tell you how wonderful you were—for every moment they are doing that they are not focusing on the other instructions, or bettering themselves, or helping each other. Put yourself in God's shoes, and think about what you would do.

What exactly is the point of worship? I ask you to consider this question deeply. Does it make you humble? Is it the embodiment of the phrase "There's always someone bigger and better."

Or does it have another purpose? Is it a reinforcement of the status and the tangibility of the thing you worship? Do you have to worship because it serves the deity or because it asserts the dominance of the thing you worship—on others?

In other words, are you worshipping because it creates humility in you? Or are you worshipping because by stating over and over again how absolutely powerful and all-knowing your deity is you are enforcing this fact on others (and yourself)? Or are you worshiping because your deity needs this worship energy?

The latter item, frankly creeps me out—it always has.

There is a difference between worship and reverence. Allow me to expand.

To *revere* something is to hold it in high regard. You can have reverence for just about anything. You can revere the craftsmanship that went into beautiful sculptures, or the self-discipline it may have taken for someone to go from being in prison to starting a business that helps kids not also end up there. You can even have reverence for the very special relationship you have with your daughter, and guiding her through life.

To *worship* something is to also hold it in high regard but then to also put it first before anything else. If you state that you worship anything other than a well known deity, you will most likely garner odd looks from those you tell this to. I'm not talking about a joke, or an exaggeration as in "I worship the ground she walks on." I'm talking about stating that you worship the squirrel that visits your yard every Tuesday, or a thing that lives in a volcano. That's odd, right? If you say that you worship a deity, and it is not a mainstream modern deity, you will also be regarded as either joking or fringe. For example, worshipping Odin, Anubis, or Zeus would be considered crazy.

However, if you worship "the god" as in "God" with whatever name you or your religion gives it, you will not typically be regarded as joking, crazy, or fringe.

However, what's the difference? I ask you this simply and naively. Surely there is a difference between worshiping God and a squirrel or a mythical deity, right? That's just offensive to suggest that. Isn't it?

What is the difference in the *act* then? Simply stated.

Remove all the rules, the congregation, the books, the hierarchy. Leave only the worship and tell me what that is exactly? Is it still a set of rules like using a hyphen when you write it, or capitalizing a pronoun? Or not using His name in vain? Those are still rules.

The more you examine this act, the more, perhaps, you will understand why I am not on board with it, and it generates that negative emotional reaction.

Again, I think that reverence is a wonderful thing—it helps us stay focused on just how important a thing is—art, engineering, perfection, our relationships—love for your wife, husband, children, grandparents. Just think about what worship means to you.

The more you examine this act, the more, perhaps, you will understand why I am not on board with it, and it generates that negative emotional reaction.

## The Big Reward

The concept of good and evil is something almost everyone can agree on (though there is sometimes debate on what acts are good, which are evil, and which are neutral). However, the concept of doing the right thing—or committing acts of good only because you believe you will be rewarded after your time is up—negates the intrinsic good of the act. The *act* may remain good, but the *intention* is negated. Being good *because you're going to be rewarded* or avoiding being bad *because you do not wish to be punished* are not acts of good or evil— they are acts of self-preservation. That's a "selfish" thing, by definition. So, all the reverence expressed, all the words that you spread are lip service as a shroud to obfuscate your simple core act of self-preservation.

So is it really selfish? If you put God first, what are you doing? You are stating that you have a set of actions—that serve you—come first before anything else in your life? They serve *you* because there simply isn't a deity that lives down the street that you can demonstrate to others. So all of your actions—good intentioned or not, as per the instruction book or based on your feelings—are self-serving. To clarify, everything you do that you say you are doing in service of God is something that you are doing in service of yourself, since you can't demonstrate the effects of your actions or interactions with God.

You may argue that feeding the poor, being humble and donating your time to others to knit blankets for the homeless are in no way a selfish act. And to that I would ask you a simple question:

***Are you doing it because it feels like the right thing to do or because you were told to and have the promise of an afterlife reward?***

If the former then it really has nothing to do with religion, because you are doing it because it feels right, not because your religion instructs you so. If the latter then it has nothing to do with being self*less* and is still a selfish act because you are doing it because of the reward.

It is immediately clear to me when someone says "I put God first" that they simply have a set of self-preservation rules in place that they put before anything else. They are selfish (consciously or unconsciously) and put themselves first. If someone is involved in their organization, then they have decided to be a part of this hierarchical structure and gain from it even further. I am not suggesting that all people who profess to put God first could not also be intrinsically good people.

If the former then it really has nothing to do with religion. If the latter then it has nothing to do with being selfless and is still a selfish act.

## A good person

Contrast all of this to someone who is simply a good person—no affiliation, not commitments to a structure, no ceremonies, and no perceived reward for their actions. Everything they do that is good is good for goodness sake. There's no worship involved. 100% of their effort goes towards what they want it to, rather than either being funneled through the lens and requirements of an organization and belief system. No additional effort is required to perpetuate and evangelize the organization—and that is what evangelism is for— not to spread the word and existence of the deity but rather to sustain the organization and increase membership. No one comes to visit, explains to you the way things are, and then just leaves. There's always that next step of membership, and membership has all the trappings we just discussed.

## Pass the collection plate

Religions are *organizations*, and organizations need funding to pay for buildings, mailings, outreach, gathering spaces, and accoutrements. Whatever form it takes, they all have a collection plate— meaning they need money from their members and as an extension—from those the members encounter. That is not to say that they don't take up collections for the poor, for projects, and so forth, but these projects require overhead and the overhead has a real monetary cost. Eventually someone becomes part of the status structure[2] built on top of the religious organization, and they are on the payroll.

All these elements that come together—worshiping of a deity (and their deputized minions/messiahs), creating and supporting an organizational unit, spreading of the information regarding the religion, attracting and initiating new members, collecting

---

[2] See "Status Structures" in *The Status Game II*.

monies from said new members, paying the members of the status structure to manage, administer and interpret what are the apparent rules and guidelines of the religion—have nothing to do with actually being good. Everything described could be (and is) applied to non-religious organizations, such as a HAM radio club or any other hobby whose members are fairly involved.

The difference is those non-religious groups— though nearly identical in structure—can only go and grow so far because they don't enjoy and benefit from tax-exempt status.

If you are a religious person then your offense to everything previously stated is duly noted.

After writing two books on status, one on inter and extra-brain communication[3], creating a card game that demonstrates dating, creating a dating site and designing a couple role-playing games, I can tell you that I am not uniquely singling out religion and spirituality. I gave equal attention to those other subjects as well.

Look, there is something wonderfully beneficial to being part of a group that, ideally, in a perfect world just wants to be good. Socialization and camaraderie and having those around you that you call friends and even family especially in times of need has a very positive effect on you and your life.

---

[3] This book may or may not be out at the time of initial publication of this book.

I'm just explaining what I think makes the most sense and feels right, to me. And, I think "good" is a concept that can and does stand on its own.

If you are a religious person then your offense to everything previously stated is duly noted.

OneSelf

# OneSelf Belief

OneSelf belief has none of the attributes described in the previous (possibly offensive to you) chapter.

OneSelf is simply an attempt to explain a belief, with the understanding that by its very nature it can neither be proved nor disproved.

## What is the OneSelf belief?

OneSelf is the belief in the possibility that you are part of a larger being.   This entity is made up of three parts with the whole being greater than the sum of its parts.  That may sound a little familiar if you have experience believing in a soul, however that's not what OneSelf describes.   Instead it is imagined that what makes you YOU is two parts—

the Lower Self and the Higher Self. The lower self is you, the person who takes out the garbage, throws up, gets sick, works out, has babies, tastes food, and has sex.

The Higher Self is the metaphysical, extra-dimensional, spiritual part of you. It's the bigger part. It controls you, but you also have free will.

Together the LowSelf and the HighSelf make the OneSelf.

Meaning, there are no other parties between you and your HighSelf—it's a one-on-one connection with no room for any of that.

To expand, OneSelf is not an organized system in which the believers gather together. That's a bit like getting other people to meet you in the bathroom to look at your reflection. This lack of system and gathering also means that there is no hierarchy. Meaning, there are no other parties between you and your HighSelf—it's a one-on-one connection with no room for any of that.

This belief concept is rather simple and easy to relay, so there is no book involved that explains the religion through parables and examples. The closest thing to that is this book—and the focus of this book is an introduction, origin and explanation.

Because this is a connection between you and your HighSelf, the need to evangelize it is non existent— you don't need to tell anyone about it because it's already happening[4]. Having knowledge about the existence and concept does not really help the process at all.

Since this isn't a club—which means there's no membership or members—this means that there is no leader. Again you don't need to elect a leader of a relationship between two entities, and that's all OneSelf is.

OneSelf is *not*:

- an organized system—there's no system; it's just you
- a hierarchy of any kind—you and your higher self, no deputized individuals interpreting what your high self is saying
- something based on a book in which you cannot ask the author for clarification[5]
- something that was established to remove your money from your pockets
- a system of rules, laws, commands—there's no

---

[4] I wrote this book because I had to; that's how writing works. I am not evangelizing.

[5] Don't get any ideas though.

list of what's right, wrong, or against the code
- a concept that requires evangelization—there's no word to spread because if it is true it exists regardless of your knowledge, and evangelization is not part of the belief system
- an organized religion—there's nothing organized about a simple concept that requires only you, and no one else
- a club—clubs are for groups, that have a gathering space
- a belief system with a leader[6]—a leader would be in place to interpret, spread, and enforce the word

OneSelf *is*:

- a self-contained concept—simple, no external forces needed regardless of who you are
- a belief of a system that is already in place—whether you are aware of it, or believe in the concept or not if it exists it simply does
- fully self-aware that it cannot be proved nor that it can be disproved—a belief system that knows it may simply not be true
- a belief that explains simply how things may work—rather than being awe and worship-based, OneSelf is about your spiritual journey
- a simple explanation for what is out there—the unknowns could possibly be explained in simple terms, without adding on additional layers

---

[6] I can hear the disagreement already.

22

Mark Bradford

OneSelf

# OneSelf has three parts

Now that you know what OneSelf is and isn't in simple bullet terms, let's discuss it in depth.

The easiest way to explain it is a video game metaphor. Have you ever played a game and called your player "your guy?" In that analogy you are the HighSelf. Your guy running around on the screen shooting stuff, or pacman or defender or the ship or the car, is the LowSelf. It is controlled by you but has some elements of free will too. Together, you and "your guy" are experiencing life. When you pause the game or save your place you go off and experience your higher life (from the game at least).

When you come back you go right from where you left off. Your guy is getting better, getting power ups, racking up score, exploring his world. You are gaining more experience with his world, and you are being affected too as your dexterity and problem solving skills increase.

In the OneSelf concept, it is similar. Your HighSelf is a what controls[7] and guides you; it has your best interests in mind because your best interests are the HighSelf's best interests. As you go through life and gain knowledge, pain, happiness, and experience so does your HighSelf.

Though your HighSelf may be guiding you in subtle and not so subtle ways, you truly have the free will to do what you want.

Sometimes things feel right—and perhaps that's when you are moving in the direction and behavior that the HighSelf truly wants. Perhaps sometimes you move in a direction that surprises the HighSelf too.

Sometimes things feel really wrong—and perhaps that's when you are going against what your HighSelf wants—and it always wants what's best for you.

## What's best for you vs. what you want

At the risk of sounding like the Mysterious Ways

---

[7] "Control" is a strong word.

comment, let's discuss what the HighSelf actually wants.  Let me ask you, if you were the supreme being in the equation, what would you want for your lower self?  Would it feel a bit like you had a child?  If it did what would you want?  If you're a parent then you know the answer—it wants what's best for you.  But what *is* best for you?  And just how *apparent* is that?

Though your HighSelf may be guiding you in subtle and not so subtle ways, you truly have the free will do what you want.

If you were born into a poor family perhaps that was the best path for you to take.  If you have certain things in your life that come easily but others that are always a struggle perhaps this is also part of the plan—the agreement.

Anyone logical immediately takes this to an extreme  and asks what about those who are far far less fortunate—being born with physical limitations,  or being born into families with addictions present, or even worse.  You can cite all the people that were born during a plague, or during the dark ages, or the witch trials, or far far worse.  What of those people?  Surely they didn't agree to this?

The answer again is that the HighSelf only works with the current environment; it doesn't directly manipulate or change it (see caretaker vs. creator). So if you are born during these dark times then perhaps your path is to navigate as best you can, to provide enrichment for when you join and become the OneSelf.

It's worth a try, and it is a very odd feeling to think that you agreed to have this stuff happen.

## The Agreement

Perhaps before you became a split person — with a LowSelf and a HighSelf — you were already the Oneself. And just before you split you made a few decisions and agreements. Could it be possible that you decided that you wanted to see what it was like to struggle with weight your entire life? What if you thought the best experience would be that of one that included overcoming poverty, oppression, or even worse? What if the most horrible of experiences were things you already agreed to? Because you wanted to experience them and this richness — however horrific — was something you wanted, perhaps even needed.

If you are the OneSelf—a being of extra dimensions, experiencing existence on an order of magnitude far greater than anything we can imagine here— perhaps those kinds of experiences are on the order of having no "extra guys" or playing on "difficult" level on a video game.

Think about that the next time life sucks. You may very well experience the horrible times quite differently with this sort of awareness. They may not suck as much, or you may be able to breathe through them.

It's worth a try, and it is a very odd feeling to think that you agreed to have this stuff happen.

You may feel empowered, you may feel special, you may even feel powerful that you've given yourself this kind of challenge.

Or you may feel like this is all nonsense—because it might be.

OneSelf

# *The Origin of OneSelf*

I was 18. This was probably one of the earliest manifestations of my "see things from an unusual angle and build/create/explain" core skill. I had experienced a lot of thoughts on deities, due partially to the world building I was doing with the role-playing games I was involved in. That experience would lead me to creating my own game and separate custom dice which were very difficult and expensive to get manufactured way back then.

I have no life-changing story regarding *religion*[8] or *spirituality*; no lightning bolt of clarity, no soul searching mountain climb, or backpacking through Europe to relay to you. It just made sense and after thinking about it for a bit I just accepted it and said

---

[8] I do have one, just not regarding religion.

"Yep, that's probably how it works."

As time went on I was part of a Catholic church, which I had an off-and-on relationship with. I renewed that relationship when I got married and raised kids. After my divorce (14 years later), now equipped with two kids full time, I joined a local small Lutheran church (which seemed like Catholic light). I taught Sunday school to little kids (a sort of co-teacher arrangement with another gentleman that became a friend) — although this teaching amounted to mostly making projects out of newspapers, noodles and glitter.

Nothing I ever saw changed my opinion and everything I experienced just reinforced my understanding of status (and status structures).[9]

Your experience may have varied considerably.

If you find this chapter surprisingly small, I don't know what to tell you. It just made sense; I kept it to myself and eventually decided to write it down, in detail very recently. And here it is. The concept is pretty simple and since there is no structural overlay, no motivation for funding, no desire to control and a blatant admission that it could all be total fiction that leaves very little to expand on as far as an origin. I'm motivated to be honest.

If you'd like to know more about my personal

---

[9] See "Status Structures" in *The Status Game II*.

experience with this there's a bit more elaboration in the chapter *The Solemness of OneSelf.* That chapter also touches on a revelation I had about OneSelf after I wrote this book.

Your experience may have varied considerably.

OneSelf

# *Horrible Horrible Freedom*

One of the interesting benefits of religion is the ability to shunt, to give up, to defer some responsibility. After all, "It's in God's hands now" and "give God your worries" and phrases like that tell us all to just give it over to a deity. In addition there's the phrase that covers all the bases and ties up all the loose ends—"He moves in mysterious ways."

That is what could very well draw many people to religion—the giving up, ultimately—of responsibility.   Isn't that one of the first considerations of joining—as well as conversely being the final straw for those that leave their religion?   Something similar happens in relationships—especially the toxic ones.   The person feels they can only do so much, and maybe they "deserve" it anyway.

Something similar could be said for the core of religions—this desire to give up responsibility, and accept that what happens—good or bad—are all things the person "deserves." No, I am not suggesting that being part of an organized religion is a "toxic relationship." I'm suggesting that sometimes people are a part of a thing for the wrong reason, or the right reason attracts them in the wrong way, or that they are part of a thing that is not benefitting them but they stay anyway because they think this is their lot in life—thus the relationship comparison.

If you worry too much you are told to hand over that worry to God, because he will take care of it. He has a plan. He knows what's best.

What if they are sort of right, with one or two major differences?

What if that higher being really does have a plan and wants what's best for you?

But what if it's *you*?

All those statements such as "My God" and "God is good" and "He is behind me and walks with me" take on a different texture don't they?

# My god vs my HighSelf

I don't know about you but my emotional reaction to such statements as "My god is great" is not positive. It sounds like the person is suggesting that they have a better connection to this infinite being, that is better than anything in the entire universe, and I am late to the party.

Think about it; if you have a causal religious commitment, or none at all, and someone uses the possessive "my" in reference to something that is all powerful, created you and everything in the universe and ultimately passes judgement on you and everyone you love, the reaction is going to be visceral and negative.

If you don't believe me, or have a committed connection to your religion try this: Imagine if someone dressed in a lot of gold tells you that "their" god is looking favorably on them. As it turns out their god is actually the Aztec god Quetzalcoatl. Your reaction would be one of amusement, right? But what if they were dead serious, and your brother, parents, half of your co-workers and half the people in your city all believed that as well?

How would you feel then? Trapped? Crazy? Left out? Would you just smile? Certainly you wouldn't say "That's crazy!" because you would be immersed in this, and these are people you care about. And, who knows, maybe a winged, feathered snake did indeed create everything and just gave your pal Linda the best day ever?

My point is that if your organized religion treats you as if you are chosen, and you speak of your deity as if it presides over everything matter-of-factly that can set up an uncomfortable situation. Check out social media and well-meaning posters to see what I mean.

Contrast that to a long time ago in which civilizations would compare their deity to the deity of other civilizations—sort of like a football team.

They still believed their deity was better and greater but they acknowledged the existence of the alternate god and gods.

It's a cognitive disconnect to think that your god is the only deity but also think that you can use the possessive "my" when referencing it.   My?  No, "the" or "our," right?

## Personal discussion

In OneSelf, the praying to fix something turns into communicating with yourself to get clarity on what is to happen next—instead of being a better sheep[10] you are being a better you.

---

[10] If you are offended by the use of the word 'sheep' then I would remind you of the phrase "God is my shepherd."

Instead of being one of billions (or very very many more if you actually believe this deity presides over the entire universe) you are one of one—this time it's personal[11].

Instead of feeling like you are just confused and one of the masses that doesn't understand, you are now empowered to take action—because that's what *YOU* want, both of you, *all* of you.

That's a freedom that religion doesn't bestow—a horrible, horrible freedom. And that's a responsibility that is now back on you—albeit you and your higher self.

# If that speaking directly to your higher self makes you feel empowered; it should.

So, if you believe in the OneSelf concept, then instead of saying "Oh why oh why did *God* do this to me?" you say "What the heck am *I* doing? What am I supposed to do with this?" and "OK, so then what can I do to move in this direction?"

If that speaking directly to your higher self makes you feel empowered, it should. You are essentially asking yourself for clarity; you are looking inward

---

[11] OneSelf—Religion, but this time it's personal. Hmm. I like that.

(or upwardly) for direction. Instead of feeling like you are letting God down, or one of many people who are part of a great audience waiting for their turn to be heard, you are communing with a higher part of *yourself.* There is little doubt that *you* wouldn't have *your* best interest in mind. It's personal.

## Killing puppies and stuff

One of the questions even devout believers in standard religion continue to voice is "Why does God do that horrible thing or allow that horrible thing to happen?" In fact there are those that become so disillusioned, so angry that this becomes their final straw, and they promptly exit their belief system because it is painful and makes no sense.

Every good thing, every bad thing that ever happened or will happen anywhere is their doing, their fault and potentially something they should have intervened in.

Maybe that's what happened to you, maybe it was the lack of lobster? Maybe you are still there and have reconciled that somehow.

Regardless, you hit on the problem with a supposedly supreme omniscient and omnipotent being—that now everything that happened is on their shoulders. Every good thing, every bad thing that ever happened or will happen anywhere is their doing, their fault and potentially something they should have intervened in. It doesn't make a lot of sense, does it? If it can do anything, and knows everything, then why kill all those puppies, why allow all those people to suffer, why allow those bad people and creatures to exist. Why did you make mosquitoes?

# Why did you make mosquitoes?

It just doesn't work and all the "God works in mysteries ways" isn't really very comforting to the people who just lost their child, or whose grandmother had to endure torture, oppression, and eradication.

If you are trying to get someone to join your club and pay the exorbitant dues in return for nothing tangible[12], you have to tread lightly on that concept, or you'll lose a lot of followers.

---

[12] I agree with your argument in advance that there is something very tangible about comfort in times of need.

## Evangelization and scrutiny

Evangelization is the act of spreading the word about your religion and your deity. Those in an organized religion are typically urged and motivated to spread this information in an effort to gain more members of the church. This push of membership is arguably one of the taxing and less desirable aspects of being part of a group such as this.

> # It's mostly all in the delivery, I suppose.

If you are non-religious and have religious people in your life, you will typically have the most adverse reaction to those with the strongest desire to evangelize.

While they consider that what they are telling you is a natural part of their belief system, it may have the opposite desired effect on you—instead of being enticed and wanting to know more you will be discouraged, repelled, and want to know less.

It's mostly all in the delivery, I suppose.

The attitude and effort put into evangelizing by a person who is part of an organized religion will vary not just by the religion but by the individual. Even those that are part of a religion with a strong evangelization mandate may still keep fairly quiet about it to others—and that is a personal choice and a reflection on personality.

Explaining your religion, the existence, and the benefits bestowed by being part of it is a bit like selling a product. In some cases, they are selling a known commodity to you; you are aware of the religion, the concepts, and may even have family members and friends who are part of it. In other cases, the commodity is unknown or at least obscure enough that indeed a level of education is in order.

However, the risk is that if the recipient has no belief in the entire concept of theism no amount of explaining, selling, and enlightening is going to make a difference— and will strain their relationship with you. It's not completely uncommon to hear that a relationship or friendship ended over religious beliefs or lack thereof. Sometimes it is the religious focus of the other person's *family*, and not the person. The word "practicing" or "reformed" is sometimes part of this conversation.

It seems disingenuous that a daughter/son/sister/ brother would hide the activities (or lack thereof) that they and their spouse participate in from their family—behaving one way in the comfort of their home, their work and friends, and then behaving another way with their family (or at least parents).
This kind of behavior and the motivation behind it seems like very valuable feedback for the religion in question, but seldom makes it to the proper people

in the hierarchy. And no one for the most part is going to re-write the book it is based on, or alter the base laws.

We use reasoning and empirical data to scrutinize everything new that we learn. To be asked to turn that off like a light switch when the subject is faith seems foolish.

So when someone decides to evangelize, there is a certain level of scrutiny. They are asking a lot from those they tell the story to and attempt to welcome into the fold.

We use reasoning and empirical data to scrutinize everything new that we learn. To be asked to turn that off like a light switch when the subject is faith seems foolish. Especially when one considers the all-encompassing nature of the subject.

If you are on the informing and selling end of it then you can expect resistance, scrutiny, and even opposition on the subject. You are not only explaining the world to them, but advising them on how they should conduct themselves. In many instances it goes deeper than that and includes their friends, family, and children. The latter can be a very sensitive subject.

In OneSelf there is no evangelization; none. If you try to count this book I will remind you that this is a book about a hypothetical belief that may or may not be true. It is one that exists or does not in complete deference to your belief in it or lack thereof.

In addition, because it is a one-to-one relationship there's no room for a "member" of a group to get involved in this spiritual relationship.

Granted, a psychologist may sometimes aid someone in getting to know themselves better, but that concept doesn't apply in the realm of OneSelf. It's just you, you, and you.

If you believe in OneSelf, then you know it is already going on for your friends and family, everyone on the planet, and everyone and everything sentient throughout the universe.

Evangelization for OneSelf is not only completely superfluous but frowned upon. Even raising awareness of OneSelf is not regarded as a necessity and in some cases could be detrimental.

As long as someone seems to be traveling along their path, learning right from wrong, doing the right thing, there's no reason to inform them of this

invisible layer.   If their devout belief in their
religion or spirituality seems to be serving them
then that could be the path they need to be on.   In
fact, regardless of what they are doing with their
life, there is no reason to enlighten them to the
hypothetical possibility.

And, since we cannot be sure of the existence of
OneSelf, there's no reason to use excessive
persuasion.  After all, maybe they are right and we
are wrong.

Evangelization for OneSelf
is not only completely
superfluous but frowned
upon.  Even raising
awareness of OneSelf is
not regarded as a
necessity and in some
cases could be
detrimental.

## Just For You

Your HighSelf is just for you. That's it. It's a one-to-one connection. It doesn't affect the weather, kill puppies, resurrect people, or flood the earth. So who does? Well, no one does, or physics, chemistry, being in the wrong place at the wrong time, and random chance. That's the environment we live in—it's not who we are. And it's not the purpose of your HighSelf.

Instead it is the natural world we live in.

OneSelf

# Mingling HighSelves

If there are HighSelves, then do they all exist together on another higher plane of existence? It stands to reason, doesn't it? And if that is so, are they aware of each other? That seems like a reasonable statement too, doesn't it? And if those concepts are both true then we have to ask the big question:

Do they talk to each other?

Think about that. Does my HighSelf talk to your HighSelf? It makes sense in the video game metaphor, doesn't it? You and I talk and we decide to play a game together. Our playing pieces don't know we know each other. And in real life we want our "guys" to cooperate too. But to them, they are just sort of motivated to help each other—it just feels right.

So what if our HighSelves operate the same way? What if my HighSelf talks to your HighSelf? What if the woman you are with—that you are madly in love with—is with you because your HighSelves chatted and said "We have to get these guys together?"

Pause for gasps.

Imagine all the possibilities, imagine all the explanations for things that have happened and not happened in your life. Imagine if that's why you met that person—*because your HighSelves already knew each other*.

Imagine further something that is a bit hard to accept—those people in your life that have done you wrong—terribly wrong—their HighSelf may be good pals with your HighSelf. Can you do that? Can you imagine that they are connected, the two of you are still connected—up there—even though he or she is an absolute narcissistic, cheating, horrible asshole.

The reason for this is that there was a need for what happened to happen. They had some sort of plan together.

Yes, the horrible divorce, the painful relationship, even the interaction that resulted in something physically harmful—all could be because one HighSelf had a need to interact with another, through their LowSelves.

Could that have been part of your agreement? Could your HighSelf have decided that this certain, life-changing, terrible thing happen to you because it was what was best? Considering this possibility could make you angry or think or both.

Again, being self-aware, if this sounds a bit like "God works in mysteries ways," it is. It could certainly be random chance, maybe there's no chatting amongst HighSelves, maybe there's no such thing as a OneSelf. That's fine. But what if there is? Interesting thought, isn't it? Kind of feels right when you meet someone great and they just sort of "appeared" in your life?

Imagine if that's why you met that person–because your HighSelves already knew each other.

OneSelf

# One Above All

So is there a One Above All? Meaning, even though everyone has their own personal deity, is there in addition to this a deity one that is above those higher selves?

Sure, why not.

It wouldn't change anything, would it?

Perhaps it would for those who are devoutly committed to their monotheist religion (just one god). But does it matter to me? No. Why? Because I simply don't know and cannot prove this. Nor can anyone disprove it. And that understanding is a mentally healthy place to be.

If you want to fit OneSelf into your existing religion, go for it. If you want to take everything I'm saying here as gospel—well, don't. That's how really bad things happen. I don't want to be responsible for a war in 300 years from now, or anyone fighting over land rights to what is essentially a desert.

If you want to disregard everything I am saying as pure fantasy, feel free.

That's the beauty of OneSelf—it is what it is whether you believe in it or not. It doesn't need you to believe in it, it doesn't need you to understand it, take it to heart or even tell other people about it. In fact I'd prefer you didn't.

## Caretaker vs. Creator

When people envision a supreme being, they often commingle the concept of a person that made all this stuff, with one that watches over us. Those are two distinct qualities; two distinct kinds of supreme beings.

When evolutionists and creationists clash, they are clashing over the *creator* concept. A lot of the talk completely ignores the *caretaker* concept. If you believe in evolution then you are focused on the universe and scientific principal creating everything. You don't even talk about the possibility that the universe is a wholly cold, scientific creation and that some caretaker deity may have shown up afterwards to get involved, complicate things, and either make the sentient life or just showed up to mess with them.

If you dispute what or who created the universe, you are wasting your time. The concept of a supreme being willing the universe into existence is equally as absurd, implausible and unprovable as the universe just showing up one day in The Big Bang[13]. How do those two things not sound exactly the same to you? Sure in one scenario a deity sticks around and waits for everyone to show up —or makes them. But the origin of the universe is exactly the same—it just shows up, out of nothing. *"Bang"* or *"Poof"* it's still a four-letter word to me.

# The concept of OneSelf is that of a caretaker deity, not a creator deity.

The concept of OneSelf is that of a *caretaker* deity, not a creator deity. The exception could be that perhaps the HighSelf does indeed create you or imbibe you with soul, but let's not go there just yet.

No, the OneSelf is there to walk with you, watch

---

[13] Yes I'm aware of the scientific proof of this, from the people who haven't left their world for another, who can't space travel, and see their own galaxy from the very edge of it. The same people that came up with "dark matter" and "dark energy" to explain the majority of the universe they can't explain.

you, mess with you, plan with and against you based on the ultimate desire for you to succeed, learn and get out of life what you are supposed to, to then return to the HighSelf and create the OneSelf.

There is an investment—a personal investment— and no time and effort spent on causing lightning to appear or waters to flood.

Mark Bradford

OneSelf

# Joining and experiences

If when you die you then join with your HighSelf, what happens then? Is it permanent? Is that what heaven actually is? My understanding[14] of this is that I don't know.

## The meaning of life

If this is all true, then the meaning of life becomes clear.

The meaning of life is for us to go on the journey we need to go on to accumulate experience and wisdom in our lives, so that we can merge this with

---

[14] That is a very generous word.

our higher self. The more enrichment we accumulate, the more we bring to the joining, and the more that benefits both our HighSelf and ultimately the OneSelf.

*In heaven there is no beer, that's why we drink it here.*

—From the song *"Im Himmel gibt's kein Bier,"* originally composed as a movie score for the film *Die Fischerin vom Bodensee*, 1956, by Ernst Neubach and Ralph Maria Siegel.

The song is about enjoying beer in our earthly forms because there is none in heaven. You experience something here because you simply cannot enjoy such a thing in the afterlife. So perhaps there is much truth to this song—that we experience things here that we cannot experience once we cross over to another place. And if we don't drink the beer or martini or take the chance, we won't bring these experiences to the being we become there.

# So drink the beer, do the thing, have the experience.

So drink the beer, do the thing, have the experience. Your experiences—good and bad, painful and delightful—are what make you you and what you hypothetically take with you.

**The more enrichment we accumulate, the more we bring to the joining and the more that benefits both our HighSelf and ultimately the OneSelf.**

## Your journey and the path

So what is your journey? Regardless of what you believe, your journey is important, and ultimately the most important thing in your life. Why? Because it *is* your life—it dictates your comfort, your fulfillment, your purpose, your happiness and your suffering. That's all your journey.

If you look at your journey like it's just unfolding before you and you are a passive viewer in a play then you're missing a great part of your journey.

If you commit to being in complete control of your journey then you are misleading yourself into thinking you have far more control over your life than you actually do—adding unnecessary stress.

So what do you do, and how do you figure out what your journey—your path—actually is? How do you walk the line between attempting to exert too much control and sitting back too passively and watching it unfold?

Have you ever felt centered? Have you ever felt in the zone? Has an experience ever felt "right?" Have you ever experienced something and felt that being in the middle of it was exactly where you were supposed to be? Those are all things, feelings, and experiences related to being on the correct path. You can meditate, talk it through, chat with others in your life, and just live in the moment. Being "in tune" with what's happening around you, and to you gives you the needed awareness to help you get on or stay on your path.

# Pain and suffering usually equal experience and experience turns into wisdom.

If you're like me then talking about a "path" sounds a little too much like pre destiny. Suggesting you have no free will is not what I intended. But, in the context of OneSelf, your HighSelf does have an intended path for you. And perhaps part of your journey is finding it. That in and of itself can be its own sort of journey. Some people struggle with "finding themselves" for most of their lives, others have "midlife crises." Others just simply pay no attention to what they are doing or even their own

Mark Bradford

concept of happiness.

But I cannot overstate the importance of the journey and the path. Paying attention to not only what makes you happy, but more importantly to what feels "right" can in no way be harmful. Just the opposite is true—you will find it a very helpful experience.

Finding your path can take reflection, meditation, experimentation, and even risk. All of those things are part of the journey we are all on. And not all learning springs from happiness, some of the most important lessons come from fear, uncertainty, and doubt. Pain and suffering usually equal experience, and experience turns into wisdom.

The more wisdom, the more you understand your path.

And just because you believe you weren't on the right path in the past doesn't mean you did something wrong, should have regret, or beat yourself up. How can you find the path if you don't walk off of it once in a while? Surely the best way to know what feels right is to give yourself (intentionally or not) a taste of what "feels wrong."

We all take a wrong turn—it's the turning back that separates being on the path with being lost.

OneSelf

# *Origins of religion and OneSelf*

If you consider what OneSelf is—a personal spiritual connection to something—you may start to muse as to whether this is the origin of other beliefs. If we feel that we are connected to something automatically, and a third person comes along and says they "know what it is and that you should just read this and hear me out..." it may sound very much like their story makes sense as a plausible explanation for this private connection we have.

If there were no religions or established spiritualities, but a lot of us felt the way that I do -that there seems to be something else—what would happen then?

What if there were no ancient tomes, and no books, no notes of any kind about deities. How long would it be until one of us spoke up? And how long until we started to compare notes and were motivated to write it down?

If someone came along and said (with a lot of certainty) that he knew what was really happening to us, and that we should all gather with him weekly to discuss it, would we? Would most of us want answers, and if these answers seemed plausible to our friends and/or family wouldn't we be pretty likely to believe as well?

It's not like your HighSelf would disagree. Or would it?

Imagine this happening a long time ago, before a lot is explained with science and meteorology and chemistry and physics. If it is a more primitive time or at least a time in which a lot less practical knowledge exists, there would be a rather large opening for explanations.

If they then go on to explain that this same spiritual connection is why the lighting strikes, the thunder happens, and the storms are present, it may all come together for you. If you add to that someone actually proclaiming to be somehow the very tangible messenger and physical manifestation of this invisible spiritual connection you may feel a very strong case is being made. Clearly this is *the guy*. You should listen to him, you think.

Add hundreds, thousands, and millions of followers

who proclaim to believe the same thing and peer pressure and feeling like you are being left out of the right thing to do can be overwhelming.

FOMO-based faith[15].

It seems to me that this is the inevitable outcome of this experiment with a group of people that feel there is something spiritual present but with absolutely no pre-written explanation.

Consider that seemingly all civilizations come up with an origin mythos. They almost invariably talk about a being in the sky—one that created, one that watches. They talk about their race being created and then managed by the one whom they worship.

But what of this? Well, perhaps the feeling of a connection is actually your connection to the HighSelf, and through the ages we have interpreted this monotheistically and polytheistically. In other words, we have interpreted this as being a connection to a number of gods that rule over and cause everything in our realities. And in some cases we have seen (and been told) that this is the cause of just one God.

Again, if we are going with a caretaker-only god— one that had nothing to do with the physical reality of the universe—then the HighSelf is just as plausible as Odin, or Zeus, or Anubis or [insert

---

[15] "Fear Of Missing Out", for those of you who are over 17 years old.

name of more modernized god worshiped here].

The belief may not *publicly* be that Modern God is not responsible for everything like the previous, more colorful deities were, but you'd be hard pressed to tell that from casual conversation—or even sermons.

Everyone from friends to neighbors to [insert title of cleric position] talk about their deity having control over the environment, circumstance, and happening.

People pray to helped loved ones who are sick, to help them get a job, to get them out of a tight jam, and to even win the lottery. "God has given us a beautiful day" and "Thank you for the food that we eat and the bounty you have given us" are all comments on the control over the physical environment.

Perhaps God did. Perhaps the physical laws of the universe that fit together to form the machinery of our existence did. The former is much more profitable to believe.

In fact learning about how the universe works— with laws that seem to be in place—starts to take more and more away from the caretaker god that messes with the environment.

It is indeed a curious thought experiment to wonder what would happen if billions of people suddenly had their memories wiped of any religious teachings but still retained all the other knowledge of science, psychology, etc.?

Would someone spring up to tell us his or her revelations, their dream, of how God spoke to them?

I am truly asking, truly curious.

Perhaps God did. Perhaps the physical laws of the universe that fit together to form the machinery of our existence did. The former is much more profitable to believe.

Perhaps our psyche, combined with our sense of importance creates this.

Perhaps it truly is God showing up and saying "Hey, tell everyone about me."

Perhaps it's the OneSelf and has always been with us.

## Spiritual maturity is an ongoing thing

First we were sure that the fire god would punish us unless we threw stuff in the volcano. Then we learned about volcanoes. Then we feared the god of thunder, and then learned about static electricity. We feared earth quakes and then learned about tectonic plates. We feared the great darkness that swept the lands and then learned about the eclipse and the planets, and our moon—called most creatively—"the moon."

The more we learn, the less we ascribe it to the actions of a deity that we have either pleased or angered.

So if we run out of things to ascribe to a god, what's left? Our own lives of course.

OneSelf is similar to this stripped down, caretaker-only belief then, but is a one-to-one personal connection to this spirituality.

It is pure responsibility with some guidance. It is communing with the higher form—one that is actually you.

Once again, the interesting thing is that if someone worships Odin or Thor or Ra, or any deity for that matter, it doesn't affect the fact that the HighSelf exists. And perhaps the path of those people includes the worship of a particular god. As I said OneSelf exists or it doesn't, and its existence is not changed by belief. Or lack thereof.

So, believe what you want—whatever works for you because if your HighSelf is really there, then it wants what is best for you.

OneSelf

# Explaining everything with OneSelf

What good is introducing a new religion (of sorts) without explaining how and why everything is actually caused by and related to it?

*"Ahh alcohol; the cause of, and solution to, all of life's problems."*

*—Homer Simpson*

One thing that absolutely all religious (and spiritual) beliefs have in common is that they can explain everything within the context of the belief system. After all, if there's no explanation for something, then your deity isn't all-knowing. If something seems to be happening beyond the control of your deity, then your deity isn't all-powerful. And remember there's always the "God moves in mysteries ways" clause to cover everything that's not explained already in cryptic self-contradictory detail.

# Since religion and spirituality really takes the form of two aspects—caretaker and creator—they all have to explain both.

Yes, each and every one of them has to take credit for and explain everything in the context of their system. And if they can't, then they adapt and expand and clarify the explanation.

Since religion and spirituality really takes the form of two aspects—caretaker and creator—they all have to explain both.

We don't.

Why? Because OneSelf isn't about a creator. If you believe in the concept of OneSelf, then you know that OneSelf is about the spiritual/caretaker aspect of life. The creation of the universe and maintenance thereof is entirely up to the laws of physics, chemistry, quantum physics, and all that stuff that Einstein went on and on about.

It's our environment and our physical reality.

The following are my understandings of common spirituality and religious concepts and how they may be explained by the hypothetical concept of OneSelf.

## Not Just Earth

Right out of the gate the OneSelf belief encompasses the spirituality of *all* people. To be more specific: *all sentient beings*. If you want to define *sentience* as *having a soul* then so be it, but you are going to have some fairly long, heated discussions about true artificial intelligence then and drawing of lines and so forth. If AI is sentient, does it have a soul? And if not then are sentience and souls two separate things, and then can something not be sentient but still have a soul? Etc.

And by all sentient beings I mean *all sentient beings in the universe*, all planets, all civilizations -everything. It means that everyone who considers themselves "one" has a OneSelf. Take that, other publications that were written before the invention of the telescope!

So it is a bit hard to envision aliens stepping off their craft, grabbing the railing with three of their tentacles, walking up and saying "Oh, yes of course, we believe that thing too—the one that only a percentage of your population believes. The one with all the violence and very, very specific verses that are completely contradictory to the formation of life in other forms, on other planets."

Right out of the gate the OneSelf belief encompasses the spirituality of all people. To be more specific: all sentient beings.

However, it's not hard to imagine that they would say that they simply believe in a higher plane of existence—one in which a part of them is already there, and they are an extension of it living here.

If they have this sort of quiet, one-to-one spirituality then the outcome of an alien visit might be a bit better, a bit less violent, and the word "conquered" and "plague" and "overlords" may not even come into play.   Imagine.

An alien race that has evolved substantially physically, mentally, emotionally, technologically, and spiritually could very well possess a belief like this (if they have any at all).

Even if they have no spiritual facet to their collective existence, the integration and relations with an alien race would be magnitudes easier if they encounter a race that simply believes in a whole spiritual self. And if this belief system doesn't dictate any aspects of life—what to wear, what to do, what not to do, what to eat, etc.—and simply is a "do the right thing and experience life" kind-of-belief then there's very little to stumble on in connecting with them.

Contrast that with aliens who pop down say hi and are duly notified that there are about 20 different religions beliefs—with one of them representing about a third of the population of the planet. Many of these beliefs in conflict with their fundamental principals.

Some have argued[16] that the existence of multiple self-governed countries—a lot of which in constant conflict—would make alien relations difficult if not impossible.

It has been further argued that perhaps it is the lack of a unified people on this planet that is what is preventing contact in the first place.

---

[16] I'm one of them.

# And if you are an atheist, the believers in OneSelf don't care; it either exists or it doesn't, and nothing you do changes that fact.

One might argue that the spiritual and religious beliefs might be even more limiting—especially those in conflict. Having 20 or so beliefs in play means that 19 of those are perhaps the "wrong" one according to our new friends, possibly overlords. Sure there's overlap, but even if one of the beliefs happens to be the same one our otherworldly pals embrace, it means that the other 19 now have to somehow convert. You don't have to take much time or effort to know that a movie based on this "mass conversion" would require that the director be Michael Bay[17].

And that's not even considering the 1.2 billion people who don't express any belief system at all. They now have to convert to (pick a random Earth religion)? How would that go?

Again, if the aliens are also those who simply believe that the physical self that we see here is an extension of a portion that we cannot see, and that

---

[17] Michael Bay makes movies with LOTS of explosions.

one day these two parts will join, there's really not much to convert to. And if you are an atheist, the believers in OneSelf don't care; it either exists or it doesn't, and nothing you do changes that fact. There's no conversion or resentment.

The visitation by a race of aliens that have a simple, non-evangelical belief is probably the most advantageous, least stressful version of this monumental event we could hope for.

And imagine if the planet they visit all pretty much believe the same thing, nonchalantly, with no judgement or requirements.

There are no churches, no religious conflicts, and no religious delegates. Instead they are greeted by whomever happens to be at the landing spot.

"Hey, sure, we believe that too, but we weren't really going to mention it because you know, it's not a big deal and in the end it's just sort of a personal thing. The universe? The formation of stars and planets? Well that's science and stuff."

## The Akashic Records

The akashic records is a theoretical master database of all knowledge—past, present, and future. It exists somewhere in a dimension that we cannot see, but although it is invisible and seemingly unreachable there are those that have reached it.

Any and all answers are there for the knowing. Everything.

Some say that various comments by Nikola Tesla and Einstein among others suggest that they found a way to tap into this repository.

Anyone who has experienced true creativity in their world can relate to this concept—because sometimes it feels like it's just coming from somewhere.[18]  If you're in "the zone," you know exactly what I am talking about—a creativity and productivity flow from you almost effortlessly.

*OneSelf*—Perhaps when we communicate with our HighSelf and do what we are supposed to it makes communication clearer and stronger.  And if what we are doing  —especially creating—is something that our HighSelf had in mind for us to begin with, then perhaps something special happens.  Perhaps this special thing is the flowing of creative energy that comes from beyond. To a lesser extent, it is the feeling of being in the zone.  To a greater extent, it is the accessing of answers—answers that are child's play to a being that is already on an expanded dimension.   See *Intuition* below for a further discussion of this.

---

[18] I have a podcast about being in "the zone" that describes this in more detail.

## Meeting The One

If HighSelves do indeed communicate, then as mentioned before it could very well be these discussions that cause them to help motivate movement in your life. Again, they are not going to make it rain because that is not their sphere of influence. But if Mary's HighSelf and Ted's HighSelf were chatting about how it would really benefit their respective LowSelves' journey to be together, one could reason that they may decide to motivate them towards each other. You could imagine Ted's split decision to visit the coffee shop on the way home in which he met Mary was because both HighSelves conspired to make that happen. The right place at the right time. She just walked into my life. Of all the gin joints... etc. You get it.

Perhaps of all these chance meetings of really important people, some of them are due to HighSelf interaction. Perhaps not. Perhaps it is all true random chance and there is no such thing. It doesn't really matter.

## Dreams

The consensus on dreams is mixed. There are those that believe that, simply, dreams are a way for our minds to "unwind" the day's events. Using its own language, the brain categorizes, checks, weighs, and stores events that happen. Combined with these events are our experiences and feelings on the matter. It is believed at the time of dreaming our minds act as a librarian putting all the books back. We have no way of tangibly and conclusively proving this theory yet.

There are those that believe that dreams are a way for us to express ourselves; things we think during the day are stored and come to life.

There are also those that think when we close our eyes we are entering another dimension entirely — one in which reality is bent by our will, we meddle with other beings and those that have passed on can sometimes visit us to give us messages.

*OneSelf* —It certainly makes sense that the brain has its own way of talking to itself.[19] We process an awful lot each and every day, including multiple media inputs (sight, sound, touch, etc) as well as the emotional sensations of happenings. The emotional impact that something has can stay with us for months, years, or even forever. Something *that* impactful has to be dealt with, lest it take over other memories—and in some cases this is just what happens to unwanted unpleasant experiences— people dwell.

There is certainly a science to dreams. Some totems do appear over and over, and some seem to follow a pattern.

---

[19] See the upcoming book from this author on this very subject.

In the OneSelf belief, there is nothing exceptionally spiritual assigned to dreams except for the following:  perhaps when we dream and are no longer processing the events and stimulus of the conscious reality we are surrounded by, we are finally free to look inward... and upward.  Perhaps at this time our communing with our HighSelf is at the most complex and intense.   Those half-formed requests, affirmations, and prayers collecting during the day make their way through the channel that is now open in the absence of any other reality. Nothing else has our attention and we are free to muse, and talk, and commune.  Our stored messages too tender and fragile and neglected during the day are now center stage.

If you look at dreams as a way to do two things you may experience less stress and a better understanding of yourself.

1. You are finally free to express yourself, so things expressed in your dreams are your way of stating your thoughts on the matter.
2. You are indeed actually chatting with your HighSelf.  This means that things you experience and learn in your dream is directly related to the path you should be on, and the results of requests you've made.

I'm not suggesting that you should always literally and figuratively follow your dreams—no.   That could be detrimental and even frivolous.    I am merely suggesting that things appear in your dreams for a reason—because you asked a question, experienced something, or planted a seed to be uncovered during the night.

Dead people visiting you? Doubtful, as they would already have merged with their HighSelves. Would another HighSelf meddle in your affairs? Probably not. Could your HighSelf generate those images, feelings, and experiences in response to something you desperately wanted to know—why not? That vividness could be the language of OneSelf.

Of course dreams could simply be a way to see things we normally can't—and we are just looking under the hood at our own thoughts as we heal at night.

## Soul

The soul is the extra dimensional part of us we carry around. For some reason I always imagined it as a smoky, semi-transparent oval shaped object that was located in the chest. Don't ask me why; that was just my brain's way of giving it form. Regardless of my imaginings, it is described in various religions as being the part of you that goes to live on when you die. In some cases it returns to a repository and returns to inhabit a body, in other beliefs it is something that goes to one of two places. And in others, it sort of goes into storage until everyone's dead—depressing!

***OneSelf*** —Since the LowSelf is an extension of the HighSelf, one could argue that we then are our own souls aren't we? When this physical body dies, we do indeed rejoin with our HighSelf. Our soul of sorts returns, rife with experiences, pains, suffering, happiness, and discoveries.

## Heaven

The concept of heaven is an infinite, perfect, amazingly pleasurable place, according to various religions and mythos. Almost all describe a place that lasts forever, in which you are happy—happier than you can imagine. You want nothing and are rejoined with loved ones. That is, unless you were bad—really bad. How bad, and to what degree this badness causes your inability to enter the pearly gates varies by religion and the person you allow to interpret said religion for you.

The belief in the soul means that the soul goes to heaven (along with all dogs, if you believe certain books and/or movies).

If you conceive of a place that is perfect, free from conflict, with all of your wants and needs and desires fulfilled, that may sound nice to some people but to me that sounds like something else: incredibly fucking boring. How do you spend a lifetime struggling, suffering, learning, seeking joy, doing the right thing (or not) and then— for an *infinite* amount of time you are on vacation. I don't want that.    My productivity, my discovery, and, even yes, some of my pains are an enjoyable part of life.    Granted I have not been here for centuries (just half of one) so perhaps after a few hundred or even thousand years I'd want to just give up and have a margarita. But forever?

A recent study showed that type A people who work really hard and then one day retire pretty much go crazy. Their world is now empty; they have nothing to work for.   Would the same be true—by a few orders of magnitude—in the case of a life lived and then retiring to heaven.

*OneSelf*—The HighSelves are doing their own thing, on an entirely different plane of existence. Much like how it is impossible for Pac Man to understand that there is more to life than eating dots, the occasional power pills, and running from ghosts, we also find it hard to imagine what exactly life is like in that new plane of existence as part of the OneSelf.  Pac Man can't imagine or relate to what it is like to crave a cheeseburger, let alone eat it.    He doesn't know about dating, marriage, a comfy bed, hot chocolate, martinis, a fist fight, throwing up, or any of the human experiences we enjoy on this plane of existence.

So, it's not surprising that we can't relate upwards to the beings that have their hands on the joysticks up there.

However, just like our lives, it makes sense that it is

not one long vacation.  Pac Man does his best to make it through the maze, embraces the power pills, and runs from the ghosts.  We do our best to get through our maze and can only wonder what the fulfilling exploded dimensions of being the OneSelf is like.  It's just not infinite bliss.  It's something else. We're probably not sitting still all the time.

The belief in the soul means that the soul goes to heaven (along with all dogs, if you believe certain books and/or movies).

## Hell

Similar to heaven, this dimension is supposedly where those souls go that were really, really bad. In some cases you don't have to actually be all that bad—you just have to cross a certain line—a line that is suspiciously weighted towards your allegiance towards the religion in question vs. personal growth or lack thereof.

## It's infinite—do the math—divide by zero and all that, people.

One of the concepts I have always had difficulty in understanding is that—like heaven—hell is infinite. And since you either go up or down, if you go to hell that means you then suffer infinitely for a finite sin. Even those that commit atrocities for their entire lives have spent an unimaginably small amount of time being bad vs. the infinite suffering existence of their time in hell. It's infinite—do the math—divide by zero and all that, people.

If your deity created this plane of infinite suffering and then sends your friends, family and coworkers there forever, how does that make you feel? Valuable? Terrified? Confused?

Let's go with "D: all of the above."

The concept of a place of suffering that is ruled by a

powerful evil being — a being whose job it is to taunt and tempt you to get you there as if he has a certain quota—is nonsensical.

*OneSelf*—There's no hell. None. All LowSelves join with their HighSelves. Can I conceive of alternate OneSelf dimensions, lost LowSelves and all that? Sure, but the point of us being here is to gather, explore, experience, and then join. Period. If you did a bad thing, then you did a bad thing. If you think I hold this belief because I have lived a fairly painless life then you are sorely mistaken; the opposite is true. Yet, I still believe that everyone rejoins and takes their good and bad with them.

## The Devil, Angels, Magical Beings, etc.

Many religions talk about beings other that God. The aforementioned Hell wouldn't exist without The Devil to rule over it —and subsequently torture said souls. There are also angels—magical beings that sometimes involve themselves in the business of man—or at least they help sell a lot of glass sculptures and posters. They also help explain why something good happens to you.

Depending on the religion there are many other beings that exist—each with their own powers and abilities. Some are people who have been granted demigod status and when prayed to, help you find the remote. No, that's a real thing.

*OneSelf*—There is the HighSelf, the LowSelf (you), and together when you join you make the OneSelf. There are no other beings with varying superpowers, mystical abilities, etc.   This is not to say that we may discover as we explore the universe beings that seem very powerful, or have what seems to be mystical, even spiritual abilities.

## Miracles

Miracles are defined as an amazing, very improbable, or simply impossible occurrence that is of a positive or helpful nature.   For those that believe in a creator god, or even a caretaker god that has control over the environment, it is logical to believe said deity was the cause of the miracle.

# We want to believe that our actions not only have consequences but also rewards.

Believing in a reward-based system—even one such as karma—can reinforce and support this belief. After all, if you believe you are doing good things, and something really wonderful and beneficial occurs that has no simple explanation, it must be caused by the deity (or flow of energy) that you believe in.  We want to believe that our actions not only have consequences but also rewards.  And, the chosen deity is all powerful, so any and all outstanding and difficult to explain occurrences that confirm our bias naturally fit into our system, and give us comfort.

*OneSelf*—If you believe in the hypothetical system of the OneSelf, then you do not believe that there is a creator deity affecting the environment, random chance, or the laws of physics. You understand that the more you follow in the path that makes the most sense, the more things may become clear—but not necessarily less difficult. You understand that most "overnight successes" have been working hard, thankless hours for sometimes more than a decade.

The reward system takes the form of cause and effect. And in the logical cause and effect a seemingly random positive occurrence usually has an explanation. Random chance, circumstances, a foundation, repetition, and other concrete tangible things are the likely cause for miracles.

Perhaps you were indeed given a chance meeting with someone because your respective HighSelves decided that the meeting was important, perhaps this kind of intervening does not happen.

## Good vs. Evil

Providing a battle supports a strong following, and being on the side of good allows for the reward system to make sense. From the primitive punishment for bad, and the sacrifice of animals to appease a god, to the doing good for karma, good and evil have an intrinsic role in religion and spirituality.

It makes sense to be on the right side. Once you believe that what you are doing is good— and righteous—there is a frightening amount of leeway allowed in your actions; history (and current events) tells us.

*OneSelf*— "Good" and "evil" are subjective terms, and each person is on their own path. Living by a moral and ethical code typically feels right. Hard work is its own reward; loyalty, commitment, kindness, love all seem to be the "right" things to do.

True moral and ethical actions are not tied to any religion nor are the the property of them. The path you are on can be difficult, challenging, and involve suffering, but ultimately the person you become is up to you. Following the path that feels right along with doing what you feel is right are both admirable. It stands to reason that the right thing to to is not always the easiest, but can garner the greatest of enrichment moving forward. This enrichment of experience and character is what OneSelf truly values. See *Heaven* and *Hell* for more elaboration of the reward system.

## The Other Side

A good portion of people believe in ghosts[20]. Their definition ranges from particular entities that just hang about and have to be chased away to loved ones that have died but their essence sticks around for various reasons. The abilities of these ghosts range from being felt to being seen to interaction with the environment to even inhabiting the body of a person to affect their actions.

> Even if it did, the
> LowSelf does not exist
> without the HighSelf,
> because they are two parts
> of the same thing.

***OneSelf***—If in theory when our LowSelf passes away there is a portion that then joins with the HighSelf could that portion for some reason stick around? The question becomes why? For what reason? In popular culture the reason is that they have "unfinished business" here, or simply do not know that they're dead. In OneSelf, the HighSelf would be more than aware that the LowSelf had passed. What if the HighSelf goes away, you may ask? Well, it doesn't. The belief in the theoretical existence of an expanded being on another plane of existence that also has a portion of itself seeping

---

[20] A recent Gallup poll says that's one in five.

into this reality does not include a lifespan for the higher being that just ends in the middle of the short lifetime of the lower self.

The HighSelf is considered to have an infinite lifespan, and that lifespan can be used for various things (see *reincarnation*).

Unlike our ever-present video game metaphor, the player does not lose interest in the character.

Even if it did, the LowSelf does not exist without the HighSelf, because they are two parts of the same thing.

Therefore, in the OneSelf belief ghosts are fascinating fiction. So the things that go bump in the night are the various materials that compose one's dwelling reacting to the change in temperature at night—or animals seeking shelter, or the fact that you propped up that bag of pretzels precariously and they fell over at midnight.

No evidence, no challenge, no empirical data has ever been presented and proven that entities such as these exist.

It's not that OneSelf belief is immune to investigation; it simply doesn't care.

You may find this to be ludicrously ironic to introduce testing and empirical data to prove or disprove something, when one could apply exactly that to any and all religions and spiritualities, including OneSelf with the same results—it's not real.

However, OneSelf is self-aware, and is a theoretical belief that could very well be nonsense, with the added bonus that even if it is true it changes nothing. It's not that OneSelf belief is immune to investigation; it simply doesn't care.

## Spirit Guides / Animals

The concept of a spirit guide is that of an non-corporeal entity that exists in another plane of existence that helps guide a human through life. Spirit Guides in western spiritualism seem to be borrowed from various American Indian tribal beliefs. These guides apparently stay with you, aiding you, guiding you, keeping you in line, and answering questions.

*OneSelf*—The concept of a spirit guide is remarkably like that of the concept of the HighSelf — communication, guidance, all seem similar. They seem to have your best interest in mind and know more about what is going to happen than you do. And they don't seem to have any control over the environment.

The difference is that you and the HighSelf are one, as all people are one with their respective HighSelves. There are no outside entities involved —the HighSelf is yours and yours alone because it *is* you.

> When I asked her, excitedly, what or who my spirit guide was she told me with a bit of surprise, "You are your own guardian."

If you want to communicate with your HighSelf and believe it is a Great Wolf that has been around for centuries, by all means do that. It sounds pretty cool to have a better spirit guide than your friend[21]. Who doesn't want that? It would make me feel pretty important to have a totem animal like that talking to me, taking an interest in me for some reason.

An interesting note is that I was once dating a woman who believed very strongly in spirit guides, spirit animals, and psychic connections. When I asked her, excitedly, what or who my spirit guide was she told me with a bit of surprise, "You are your own guardian." She went on to say that it is

---

[21] I'd have a dragon, Kirin or gryphon. Look them up.

extremely rare but it does happen from time to time.

I suppose in the OneSelf belief I am indeed my own guardian, and so are you and everyone else.

## Reincarnation

A number of religions believe in the concept of reincarnation. Instead of releasing your soul permanently to another plane of existence (heaven, etc), those that are reincarnated are only staying there temporarily. The length of stay may not be very important, but the fact that the souls returns again to physical form is. So for some religions, this may be the third time you are back, or the fiftieth, or more.

One of the major tenets of a religion practiced by over a billion people is that this returning to a body happens many many times over. In fact there's nothing stopping the soul from inhabiting something other than a person—it can indeed be an animal.

Perhaps it is the experience the OneSelf already had that helps guide and color your world a bit.

*OneSelf*—Since the purpose of the LowSelf is to experience and explore and bring that experience back to the HighSelf as the OneSelf, and since there's only so much one can explore and accomplish in one lifetime it is conceivable that this process could be repeated. Why not? Perhaps it is the experience the OneSelf already had that helps guide and color your world a bit. Perhaps you are so adverse to people who are lazy because your previous LowSelf was really lazy. Or maybe it's just your childhood. Like all parts of the OneSelf belief, it is what it is.

However, are hamsters sentient? Just how much experience are you garnering running on a wheel spending most of your time eating the same food and pooping in wood shavings.

## God

Most religions describe a god that is above all else. He[22] rules everything and is both omniscient and omnipotent.

*OneSelf*—*See One Above All* chapter for details and expansion of this.

---

[22] Or she or it. Regardless of the pronoun you are supposed to capitalize it.

# The Universe

There has been a movement lately to refer to the universe as an entity. People consider the universe to be a sentient all-knowing, all-powerful being. Why not? It's so big, full of so much and by its very existence it's been around the block a few times. If something exists, it's IN the universe. If something happened, then it happened IN the universe.

Essentially those that use "Universe" instead of "God" are just replacing one word with another. The benefit of this is that by using "universe" you appear to be approaching it from a scientific perspective. The universe is religion/belief/deity agnostic (no pun intended) so you don't have to worry about association to a specific religion. Even disparate spiritual beliefs can still all use "universe" without associating with their counterparts.

*OneSelf*— The universe is an amazing, incredible, awe-inspiring reality. It's the playground, the environment, the *everything* we get. However it is not sentient, any more than a building or a park or the horse head nebula is[23]. If you are going to ask "The Universe" for something you are essentially asking "God" for something. If you do, then you run into all the problems of a single, omniscient being watching over countless trillions of sentient life forms.

---

[23] As of this writing, of course.

# Essentially those that use "Universe" instead of "God" are just replacing one word with another.

And if you think the universe has control and isn't just passively listening, then you run into the caretaker problem in which this one single thing is not motivated to intervene in your life. Pulsars that can wipe out entire planets, colliding galaxies, black holes the size of galaxies and you think it cares if Karen and you are having a problem?

The universe, when referenced as The Universe, is Generic Omnipotent, Omniscient God. And that's fine if it works for you. Perhaps The Universe rules over all the HighSelves, perhaps not.

## Suicide

Most religions and spiritualities frown upon taking one's own life. Some of them outright forbid it. In some, there is an indifference to it that has only changed in modern times (with their instruction manual openly discussing it without repercussions). Some spiritualities believe that what you do in one lifetime reflects upon, colors, and alters the next (see *reincarnation* above).

*OneSelf*—There's a very distinct connection to the video game metaphor when it comes to suicide. If we imagine that you are the video game character and your HighSelf is the player, then taking your life is tantamount to you ending the game—that shouldn't be possible in a video game. The character does not simply die for "no reason." It is almost always because of his actions within the context of the game. And, in the OneSelf belief the "context of the game" is the environment we live in which—just like the video game—the player has no real control over.

So ending one's life and thus ending the game is both unfair to the player and the HighSelf. Thus it is not acceptable in the OneSelf belief.

Remember that as the player you can see far more than what your "guy" is immediately experiencing, and having played the game before you know what to expect. So a seemingly desperate situation for you may just be a short pause for your HighSelf who sees a really fun time (and many years of experiences) ahead.

Since the LowSelf (you) is not just a playing piece randomly awarded to the HighSelf, but rather an extension of it, this means that the ending of one's life is not just the premature ending of the experience for the LowSelf, but it is also for the HighSelf. Does this mean that all HighSelves are active participants in the decision, the feeling, the finality, and final push to end one's life? Does it stand to reason that if the LowSelf is an extension of the whole then the whole must feel this way? Further examination of this reveals that it does not.

# Looking at one's life as an experience–good or bad, pleasurable or painful–dictates that one must continue with the experience.

Could it be possible that the experience of giving this ultimate control over the game is the experience the HighSelf was looking for? Perhaps, though it does seem self-limiting. The same could be said for those who experience short lifespans due to medical reasons or misfortune.

Taking an active role sets it apart, however.

Looking at one's life as an experience—good or bad, pleasurable or painful—dictates that one must *continue* with the experience.

How does mental illness play a part in this? How does it play a part in the human experience, the LowSelf experience, and ultimately the OneSelf?

Perhaps mental health—or lack thereof—was simply an option to be taken or not. Does this seem callous? In a way the entire discussion of OneSelf could seem that way, as it looks at the entire experience of a life (or more than one) as simply a journey of experience.

There's no comfort in that, except in believing that mental illness, misfortune, pain and suffering are all experiences of the LowSelf, not the HighSelf. However, that experience is something that enriches and manifests in the eventual OneSelf.

"Mental illness" is a conveniently simple way to describe a very complex spectrum of issues. I'm being equally as conveniently simple in addressing it here, admittedly.

The bottom line is that in the OneSelf belief it is better to have the experience than not to—unless that lack of experience *is* the actual experience.

## Prayer

Most people have prayed at one time in their life; some people pray all the time. Prayer is an integral part of almost all religions, and a form of prayer exists in most if not all spiritualities.

When someone prays they are essentially "talking to God" whatever their god (or gods) may be. It is a way of communicating by thinking words and phrases. These words and phrases take a few forms:

*Affirmations*—Some people talk to God and just repeat that they are a good person and that their actions are positive. They are essentially talking to God just to make sure that he's aware of why something was done—even though it's believed he is all-knowing. Why not be sure?

*Questions*—When life is a little complex or something happens that makes no sense, those that pray ask God questions. Sometimes the questions are gentle questions about something that happened; other times they are full of emotion as in, "Why, why, why did you do this to me?!"

Some ask questions and wait for an answer in the form of a sign; others just keep asking questions over and over again.

In traditional prayer, asking a question can feel a bit like taking a number in a long line or submitting a question to a publication or even entering a lottery.

You can feel that you are just one of many. "He moves in mysterious ways" is a typical good response for those that ask and receive no clarification.

*Requests*—When you don't get what you want, you ask God for it. These requests can range from a slight tweak to how things are going —"A better day than yesterday" to an outright ransom note-like request "If I don't get this job, then that's it!" Sometimes those that are at their wits end also include a threat to stop believing entirely. This may happen multiple times.

***OneSelf***—If you are a lower part of a whole being, and you want to communicate to the higher portion, are you praying? If you are, are you praying to yourself?

> You are no longer one of millions or trillions making a request to a singular all-powerful deity. Instead you are talking to yourself.

Prayer takes on a very different meaning if you believe that is true. You are no longer one of millions or trillions making a request to a singular all-powerful deity. Instead you are talking to yourself.

The prayer can—and does—still take on the forms mentioned previously (affirmations, questions, and requests) but the system is a bit different.

*Affirmations*—Repeating affirmations to your HighSelf means you are clarifying your actions and verifying that what you are doing is in line with your character, your desires, and your journey as a whole. In that way, it is more similar to affirmations said into a mirror than traditional prayer. "I've given this a lot of thought, and I feel good about this decision."

*Questions*—Asking yourself a question is a bit different than asking a deity. You are aware that your HighSelf is not answering questions for anyone else. Your OneSelf does indeed have something to gain from you understanding the answer, or even considering the question. That is not to say that those that believe in the OneSelf concept will have all questions answered; no it means that having the attitude that perhaps some of the answer comes from you makes it an entirely different experience. And the "you" in the equation can be both your HighSelf and the person reading this. In other words, the answer may indeed be right there. That's a different feeling than being part of a crowd and feeling a bit lost and hoping your number comes up. The level of personal responsibility increases, in a good way.

However, it makes more sense that a being that is actually you would have the motivation to help in the journey without actually changing the experience.

*Requests*—Since we understand that your HighSelf is a one-to-one connection with you—and is a caretaker entity that has no control over the environment—requests are limited. Meaning, you are not going to be asking your HighSelf to make it rain or cause someone's health to improve or allow you to win the lottery.

Granted, a being of extra-dimensional depth, of expanded dimensions that has the depth and breadth of understanding that we cannot comprehend could indeed understand random chance to the point that it is no longer random, or comprehend weather so that predictions are better than a "60% chance," or health to the point as to make healing seem like magic. Your attitude and thoughts do indeed affect your health. A recent study shows that the "placebo effect" is not a trick of the mind but a cause of the mind. And mental health and stress play an important part in physical health.

However, the aforementioned being is not going to intervene in the environment, unless of course the environment is actually being controlled by a LowSelf in some way.

Regardless, OneSelf requests take the form of being able to do something or not failing or having an obstacle removed.    In many ways, they may be similar to requests made in prayers.    However, it makes more sense that a being that is actually you would have the motivation to help in the journey without actually changing the experience.    And perhaps that is the essence of the relationship between you and your HighSelf.

"Let's do this."

Perhaps the answer to a request or question or affirmation comes in the form of a feeling. Perhaps the answers never really come, and perhaps the absence of the answer *is* the actual answer. Seems like I have all bases covered with that statement, doesn't it?

Meaning, you are not going to be asking your HighSelf to make it rain, or cause someone's health to improve, or allow you to win the lottery.

Regardless of that, the answering of a question is not going to be in the form of noodles arranging themselves to form a word, or all the animals at the petting zoo suddenly, softly, saying your name[24]. Instead it's going to be a "gut feeling" or just a bit of intuition, or perhaps a lack of fear.

This, of course, could be and probably is caused by you just mentally and emotionally coming to terms with something.

See *What Now?* for my personal experience with this, and the revelation I had in writing this book.

## Luck

The more you believe in luck, the less you believe in deities—they are not compatible. That is of course unless the concept of luck is co-opted by a religion to demonstrate how the deity or various entities are intervening in your life on positive and negative levels you cannot explain.

> *"Chance favors only the prepared mind."*
>
> *—Louis Pasteur*

---

[24] When I was 11 I swear a door slowly creaked open and said "Maaaark." That would have been much more impressive if my name was "Leonardo."

So if you believe in a certain level of luck (meaning, anything but none), then you ascribe happenings in your life to something you can't control, can't explain, and believe is real. There's a certain level of frustration if this luck is bad, and it may reinforce your beliefs if this luck is good.

*OneSelf*— The description above of "you ascribe happenings in your life to something you can't control, can't explain, and believe is real" is an apt description of OneSelf. If you are experiencing what you believe are these happenings and they seem outside random chance, you could say that they are the effects of a HighSelf. Perhaps this good stuff is because you are moving in the proper direction and your HighSelf continues to align things properly for you.

If you experience bad luck, it may be that you are going against the current of desires of the OneSelf as a whole, so things just "don't work out."

Or perhaps Louis Pasteur is right?

Or perhaps the quote above is relating the tangible effects of going in the right direction?

The description above could easily be used by a mainstream religion (or any for that matter) to explain luck.

So, if you believe in a certain level of luck (meaning, anything but none) then you ascribe happenings in your life to something you can't control, can't explain and believe is real.

Regardless, doing things that seem to be in the "right" direction often results in positive outcomes.

But, from someone whose motto was (for a while) "No good deed goes unpunished" I can also attest to the opposite.

Your experience may vary and probably does.

## Intuition

Intuition is said to be the understanding of concepts and things without consciously reasoning through them. Expanding on this, we can say that a part of your brain understands something before you do. Something deeper than conscious surface-reasoning is at work. It could simply be a brain language hierarchy at work in which lower levels of cognition are processing—much in the way that a "hunch" is more than just a feeling. Referred to as "instinct" or your "inner voice[25]" it is a part of your decision-making process.

*"But instinct (intuition) is something which transcends knowledge. We have, undoubtedly, certain finer fibers that enable us to perceive truths when logical deduction, or any other willful effort of the brain, is futile."[26]*

*- Nikola Tesla*

We have no definitive tests or data measuring intuition in an empirical fashion, but intuition is something we deal with all the time, is spoken of

---

[25] More on this in another book.

[26] Chapter III, "My Inventions: The Autobiography of Nikola Tesla"

repeatedly by all manner of speakers, leaders and those to whom we look up to. Intuition is a thing.

As I mentioned in *The Akashic Records* above, both Tesla and Einstein have mentioned receiving guidance and information from a source they can't define. They were both very aware of the absolute importance of intuition. For all of their inventions, equations, science, and math, they valued inspiration higher. And so should you.

Their inspiration was not of the "I shall take up a sword and crusade" variety. No, it was an inspiration that allowed them to pursue complex and heretofore unheard of, ground-breaking concepts. And they were tangible concepts that the entire world has benefitted from. We are talking about men of science—hard science—that valued an intangible thing above all else, because it was a fruitful experience with more depth than simple problem-solving. Both Einstein and Tesla have numerous verified quotes about the merits of intuition and receiving information, data, and guidance from an external source.

# Perhaps intuition is a word for something that has no form, in a language we do not speak.

*OneSelf*—Again, it is not at all uncommon to hear that various religions assign all inspiration, intuition, and guidance as coming from their deity.

The difference with OneSelf is that it is essentially coming from you—but of a higher portion of you that is "in-tune" with the universe. And that description matches very closely what others use to describe looking inward to manifest creativity, inspiration, and other energies.

Perhaps intuition is a word for something that has no form, in a language we do not speak. Perhaps intuition is the language we speak with our HighSelves.

Regardless, it is a wonderful thing to experience. The more you enrich your ability to experience (and act on) intuition, the more you will feel that you are on your path.

## Karma

People get this wrong, a lot. I'm not speaking about the OneSelf equivalent; I'm referring to those that believe in karma in general. When people think of karma, they think of it as a positive or negative energy. To them, it's a sort of list of good and bad actions that accumulate negative and positive points. They think that if you do a bad thing on the way to work—say, cut off another driver—that on your way home it's likely that someone's going to cut *you* off because *karma*. The problem is they are wrong; that's not the actual definition of karma. Karma is multi-incarnational. What I mean by that is that your actions in *this* life, affect your results in the *next* one. That's according to the writings of the people who actually introduced the word.

*OneSelf*—If indeed the joining of the LowSelf with the HighSelf occurs more than once, then there is reincarnation in OneSelf. Perhaps the absorption of skills and knowledge and happiness and pains and experiences is too much for just one lifetime. Perhaps the cycle of learning and joining and enriching happens many times. Perhaps it happens an *infinite* amount of times? Like our video game metaphor, perhaps the player not only wants to play the game over and over but also try other games? In that case, it could be conceivable that in your last lifetime you were a child of another country or even another planet. Maybe you can only learn so much with our kinds of brains, breathing this oxygen-methane mixture, and walking upright? How much are we missing by not being part of a culture that floats in the sky or huddles together next to a vent at the bottom of an ocean of liquid methane?

In some instances of the reincarnation belief, it is understood that there are levels. Again, a great video game metaphor. Your guy gets better as you play, levels up, adds stuff, and becomes a greater being.

# This "old soul" you know has joined with a higher self, then come back again more than once with all the experience, albeit not the knowledge.

What if we also move through levels? It's not unheard of in some beliefs to start out as a lowly creature and then be reincarnated into a greater and greater animal, culminating into Congratulations You're A Human.

The term "old soul" can mean that the person has been around a long time—far longer than one lifetime. So even if there aren't any animals involved perhaps an old soul has joined with their HighSelf multiple times. An interesting thing to think about it, yes? This "old soul" you know has joined with a higher self, then come back again more than once with all the experience, albeit not the knowledge.

Perhaps you feel like you're an old soul?   If so, does this description of what it actually is make a lot of sense to you?   Does it feel plausible?   If spirituality, another plane of existence and organized religion all sound plausible then this is probably no different.

It's probably not much of a leap of...

OneSelf

# Faith

## Faith is many things

The commonality with all religions (and most, if not all spiritual beliefs) is the concept of faith. Faith, as was previously stated, is the belief in something without the tangible proof. The meaning is often stretched to encompass multiple things. It is sometimes used to describe the belief in a deity or a final resting place like Heaven. With essentially no proof other than anecdotal evidence, emotional stories and fiction you are asked to believe in a thing[27]. It is also used to describe something a bit milder—believing in a person or thing to perform a task or behavior. Meaning, that you should have faith that your friend will do the right thing or that a

---

[27] I'm not suggesting whether that is good or bad.

business will come through with your unusual vacation request or even with a refund from a product. Seems like an awfully wide meaning for the same word, does it not? A life-long belief in another plane of existence that you will one day take up residence in for an infinite about of time should *not* have the same weight and meaning as hoping that your friend will pick up up at the airport on time this time.

Yet that's what faith is, in very broad terms.

So it would seem that regardless of religious beliefs or spirituality, we all experience and participate in faith. I use "participate" because it is an active thing by its very nature. If you have no faith, it goes away. If stuff happens in your world and you either think nothing of it, don't ascribe magical mystical origins to it, or you simply believe that they happen because of provable cause and effect, then you're not participating in faith.

## Faith in Groups

Faith is better in groups. If you get a group of people together for almost any purpose, it enhances the experience of the purpose. There's almost always a core group that puts effort into maintaining the original purpose of the group—the 80/20 rule in action. Then there are those that are there for moral support (the 80%). And then there is that guy that shows up and ... why does he keep showing up?

# ...because a lot of what faith is composed of is essentially moral support.

Faith groups have the advantage of benefiting from those that are just there for the moral support—because a lot of what faith is composed of is essentially moral support. If someone can offer support, encouragement, and even anecdotal evidence to support your common faith, the experience is that much better. Faith is reinforced, you are assured, and you don't even mind that one guy that shows up because he believes too and well, that's OK.

Additionally if you are a member of a faith group, and most if not all religions or spiritual beliefs are group-based—you get a church or a yoga mat after all—then you can exit the group without exiting.

Depending on the stringency of the requirements, you can completely lose faith with the belief system and still be part of a faith group. Remember that there are usually a number of individuals who are part of the 80 of the 80/20 rule. They already have diminished or really no faith at all[28]. If you are a member of an organized religion and take strong

---

[28] This isn't a guess; this information is based on heart-to-heart discussions I've had with members of a congregation.

exception to that, then you are a member of the 20%, obviously. If your reaction is more one of casual acceptance, then you're part of the 80%[29].

Or maybe you're that one guy?

Regardless of which player you are, you're going to benefit from the collective faith of the group, even if you lose yours.

## Misery loves company

This benefit is because there are others that are already there—in a state of lessened faith, doubt, or even complete lack thereof. And they stay because of reasons other than faith. As social animals requiring validation[30], humans quite enjoy being a part of the right group. If you feel that you are part of a good (faith) group of people, then losing faith is not only common but causes little or no change on how you participate. The majority of those that belong to a group such as this typically do the minimum —showing up, perhaps paying dues when required, etc.

Note again that faith groups range from devout sects to a weekly yoga class—they all have a certain

---

[29] Obviously it doesn't break down to exactly 80/20 but most people are familiar with this rule, and it's a way to explain that the minority carry the weight of the faith, and the others are there just for the refreshments.

[30] See "Validation" in *The Status Game II*.

amount of faith. If you dispute that and suggest that Yoga is simply stretching, then you are missing the point, and your yoga teacher is actually teaching a spin class.

Most individuals have had a fairly similar experience with their chosen religion —a diminished interest, a continued participation based on assumptions, and perhaps a bit of guilt and obligation. In the end they continue to do it because of the aforementioned emotions. And they stick around because it is in line with their various motivational gages.

But the faith is gone. And that's OK.

## The (in)equality of faith

It's very attractive to believe that in being a part of a group you will be equal to not only the group, but everyone. Faith, on the surface, does that. If your faith is one of popular modern organized religion, then you are told that you are one one of many, and that all of his creations are not only equal, but special and even made in his image.

That is until you get more involved in the group, then you will find that there are those that hold a higher position. You then must ask yourself, why are they able to hold this position and deliver (and more importantly *interpret*) the word? Why do we listen to what they say instead of what the deity says? Since we can't actually hear the deity speak and it doesn't communicate with you directly[31], then we must rely on what is written. But the written word is not enough, so attending a church of some kind allows these people in higher positions to read the word aloud to us.

There are some possible risks involved in that, however. Since most people don't read the written word themselves, they don't bother to go back and check on the accuracy of what is being read and what has been written. Since a lot of what is written was typically written a long time ago, it leaves a lot of room for interpretation and modernization. In addition, most sermons are based on reading a small passage and then greatly expanding on that, thus, once again utilizing the 80/20 rule. In this case, it is 80% interpretation, modernization and personalization and 20% verbatim written instructions.

# We are all flawed, just some more than others, says the person who holds a position of power over you and your family.

This interpretation leaves a tremendous amount of

---

[31] I understand that you may say it does once in a while, but even that is a tiny fraction of the word being given to you.

room for variance, and that variance can take the form of misinterpretation or intentional hijacking to serve the needs of the individual or organization, hypothetically of course.

So though you are initially told that everyone is the same, created with the divine spark, and equal, you quickly learn that your are not so equal. This belief, combined with your doubts or even actions you regret, can drive the point home in a most impactful way.

We are all flawed, just some more than others, says the person who holds a position of power over you and your family.

In OneSelf we are all who we are, whatever that is. You are the LowSelf of your HighSelf and will one day recombine to be the OneSelf. We all will do that. In that way, we are equal. In other ways, we are not. Some of us are jerks; some of us are amazing. Some of us are really attractive, and some of us are schlubs. It may be our choices; it may not be.

HighSelves don't write books; LowSelves do. Advice from other LowSelves can be useful, but control over your life should not be handed over lightly, especially if it is in exchange for an infinite reward. For those that wield that kind of power over you can literally control your life and your actions.

Free will, or at least the wonderful illusion of it, and the horrible horrible freedom that comes with it, is preferable.

## Unwavering Faith

Do not come away with the impression that I am suggesting that all religions and spiritualities are made up of only a tiny fraction of people who actually believe. No, and I'm not suggesting that in an attempt to shake your belief or describe a house of cards. I am suggesting that the 80/20 rule probably does apply to churchgoers and other faith-based groups (and really all groups). And that people who belong to these groups have lost some or all of their faith at some point. However, there are those that seemingly have an unshakable faith. Those that have this zealousness have a faith that seems almost so strong as not to be a faith—for it seems almost like knowledge. What of those people? Well, good for them. My personal opinion is that if you're not hurting anyone then I do not have a problem with it. You're welcome to have whatever discerning, discriminating beliefs you like —again as long as you're not hurting anyone. And that's my opinion. However, the OneSelf belief has two very important points on faith.

## One Right makes the rest Wrong

OneSelf is the belief that there is a higher self.

Since we can't prove that it *is* truly a faith, in that way, OneSelf is similar to other religions and spiritualities.

However, what would happen if somehow we were able to prove the existence of this other part of our selfs—the existence of Heaven, of God, and the aspects that make religion and spirituality faith-based? What if we were to prove this, scientifically, measurably, provably with empirical reproducible demonstrable data?

What happens to the religions if faith is no longer required? If instead religion became more a series of instructions more like a documentary? Facts?

Some religions would benefit, while others would be slightly diminished. For some, it would be a culture shock. And since most if not all religions are mutually exclusive it would not really be possible to prove them all right—most have their own specific god, messiah, and mascot. Some are monotheistic (there's just one God—theirs), while others are polytheistic (they have a number of gods, each with their own purpose—like Ptah, the Egyptian creator god vs. Ra, the god of the sun), etc. Even modern religions are for the most part mutually exclusive. So if in our hypothetical thought experiment of finding scientific data that one is right, it would work best if just *one* was proven right.

It just doesn't work to prove that more than one is

right. Because they all can't be right.

Well, unless it is OneSelf.

## Faith doesn't matter to OneSelf

If you were to prove that yes indeed a part of us is currently living on another, expanded plane of existence and that when we die a part of us—our experiences and hopes and dreams and pains and suffering—all exist beyond the physical and join to make a new being what would happen then to those that believe in this particular system?

Well, nothing.

# Data does not diminish or erase faith–if it did then no religion would have survived to this day.

If you believe in the hypothetical concept this book introduces you to and it is indeed proven scientifically to be correct, your reaction would be the same as everyone else that believes it—

"Hmm, well, there ya go."

That's because *faith doesn't matter to the OnSelf belief.* It's not the driver, the hook, or the reward.

It just is. It may be right, and it may not be. If it's right, then you just keep going and perhaps at most you might be a little more motivated to do the right thing and seek out experiences. If it's right, then you'd still not have a problem with friends and family that believe in something else (because the alternate belief might be something their HighSelf wants them to explore). And, even with scientific data proving that OneSelf is correct and real, those of other belief systems would not really be affected. Why? Because of faith. Data does not diminish or erase faith—if it did then no religion would have survived to this day.

Data to prove or disprove it does not affect it, except on the very, very most obvious of levels. Granted, it would be difficult to find someone who believes in a chair that floats above Hawaii and grants wishes to those that disavow toothpaste and put clamshells on their doorsteps once a year.

## OneSelf is not tribal. Faith does not affect OneSelf. It is or it isn't. It is right or it's not.

Or equally as difficult to find are those that believe that throwing old dishes into a volcano appeases The God of Ceramic.

But tune down the absurdity a bit, and you hit a wall. No amount of data in either direction (proving or disproving) will shake the faith of some. Why? Because it is *the faith itself* that keeps them coming back. It's the validation[32], the feeling of belonging, and of being a tribe.

OneSelf is not tribal. Faith does not affect OneSelf. It is or it isn't. It is right or it's not. Even if it's right, it doesn't preclude the participation or even the devout belief in a different religious system.

The faith in it doesn't bind us together because there's no *us*, no congregation, or no group. It's a one-to-one personal relationship, if it exists. It's YOU and you.

## Cottage Industries

It would be a bit naive to think that even though this is a one-to-one private connection, that in the event this concept catches on, a number of capitalistic businesses wouldn't spring up. People telling you that they can "coach" your spirituality and that if you read their book they can enhance your experience would surface. You'd even see those that can "channel" your HighSelf to give you a clearer understanding of what it wants (they can't). Those would appear too.

---

[32] See "validation" in *The Status Game II*

# Again, if OneSelf exists then none of that matters to your ultimate journey.

Is this bad? Yes. Is this good? Yes. Does your HighSelf care? I don't know, ask it; how does it make you feel? That may be your answer. Again, if OneSelf exists then none of that matters to your ultimate journey.

Maybe it would be fun to experience someone who thinks they can help you with your journey with it. Maybe it would even be fun to waste tens of thousands of dollars[33] in the pursuit of having someone channel your HighSelf. Maybe it would be a horrible waste of money. That's up to you. OneSelf as a whole doesn't care. And your HighSelf doesn't either. Unless it does, and your journey is to uncover this.

I tell you this to make you aware of the possibility, because it is certainly inevitable, isn't it? Just see it for what it is, and expect all the wonders of capitalism and opportunistic behavior.

---

[33] I would suggest you direct that towards me, for purely selfish reasons.

OneSelf

# Happy Holidays?

According to pew research[34], over 90% of Americans  (that's nine in ten for those that don't like percentages) celebrate Christmas.   That easily qualifies as "most people."   Interestingly, 45% of those that celebrate Christmas celebrate it from a religious perspective, verses a cultural one.

As an example, Christmas is something most people celebrate, and only half celebrate as part of a religion.

In other words, for half of those celebrating it is a secular holiday — no religious aspects for them.

So what's left?  Well, all the fun aspects like getting

---

[34] http://www.pewresearch.org/fact-tank/2017/12/18/5-facts-about-christmas-in-america/

together with families, the gift exchange, minor mythos like Santa and St. Nick, etc.

We can agree that a lot of people celebrate some religious holidays because it's a holiday, and they value family and friends and the celebration without perhaps any religious or spiritual attachments added.

I'm not picking on Christmas. I love it, for all the reasons above. In the OneSelf belief, something that brings people together, celebrates friends and family, and is an excuse to drink together can't be bad.

# I still want the deviled eggs, the hot chocolate, and have always had fun playing Santa.

And, as always, if your belief system dictates the religious aspects of Christmas, or any other religious holiday by all means celebrate it. Those that are part of the hypothetical belief system of OneSelf appreciate that.

I still want the deviled eggs, the hot chocolate, and have always had fun playing Santa.

Your participation and belief in your particular holidays is part of your journey.

It fits within the OneSelf belief, if OneSelf exists, of course.

OneSelf

Mark Bradford

# The Solemness of OneSelf

OneSelf is a personal belief in a one-to-one connection between a lower being and a higher being, in which the experiences of the lower being enhances that of the higher being when they join, creating the OneSelf.

Because this is a one-to-one connection, there's no arbiter between the "deity" and the "follower."

Your "god" is not my "god." And vice versa.

Because OneSelf is believed to exist regardless of whether you believe in it or not, there's no reason to evangelize and "spread the word." I don't need to tell you about something that exists already, that doesn't require you to worship it, and is a personal connection.

Because the HighSelf is looked upon as a personal caretaker being vs. a creator being, we never ascribe external happenings to it. We don't thank it for the rain or curse it for the earthquake. We don't pray to it to make sure the sick get better.

*Sidenote*—appreciation and gratitude are never bad things. By all means be appreciative and thankful for the things you have in your life—the wonders of nature, the smile in your child's eyes, the indescribable feeling of holding hands with the one you love. I want to make that perfectly clear here. Gratitude is an amazing, cleansing, important thing. Lack of entitlement is what removes the filters from your perception. This is so important I interrupted the train of thought being made here. Let's continue...

However, we might ask about understanding something better, being able to tolerate a certain challenge, or anything else that could possibly be under our/their control. What you ask, what you rant about, what you scream at your ceiling that makes your cat think you are angry at it—that's entirely up to you. Think, pray, talk, rant, laugh —it doesn't change anything, except maybe your mood, and your understanding.

And finally, because there is a certain self-awareness of the possible absurdity of all this, someone who believes in the hypothetical possibility of the OneSelf concept does not insufferably discuss it with others[35].   Your OneSelf journey is distinct and different, but just as important as the OneSelf journey of your friend or lover or kids or the person that murdered three people last week[36].

# Over 30 years have passed and I've never mentioned it to anyone.

There's no conversion.    There's no "seeing the way" or the "light."   It's already happening.   An awareness of it is simply... interesting.

Because of all of this there is a certain quietness to OneSelf—a certain pleasant solitude.  Again, there's nothing aloof about it as OneSelf is not better; it just is or isn't and that's enough.   Perhaps solemness doesn't apply perfectly as it suggests a seriousness, and that is one missing aspect that definitely sets it apart from other belief systems.   Paradoxically the less you take life (and yourself) seriously the more you get out of it.  "Don't sweat the small stuff" tells us that there are little things in life that aren't important.    When you look at everything as a whole, and know that you don't have all the answers, you realize that it's possible not to sweat

[35] I fully accept that label here if you choose to give it to me, even though I have done my darnedest to not appear that way.

[36] A shocking statement, to be sure. It doesn't diminish the horror of the atrocity, but it is what it is, in the truest sense of the phrase.

anything while putting tremendous effort into making sure the outcome is to your liking. That's confusing, misleading, and annoying. But it's true. The moments in which we remember that paradoxical truth are our best moments in life. When all looks dark in your life, and you sit down, shake your head and say out loud, "Holy shit am I screwed" what happens next determines your sanity and your success. Because, if you then just start laughing at the absurdity of everything that's when you get it.

I theorized that OneSelf was a thing, and myself started quietly appreciating it when I was only 18.

Over 30 years have passed and I've never mentioned it to anyone. 30 years.

# Because of all of this there is a certain quietness to OneSelf—a certain pleasant solitude.

In all that time, I've thought about it, tested it (as one can test a theoretical unprovable thing), and carried it with me. I've mused about my HighSelf vs. God. I've thought about personal development and my journey. I have considered the journeys of my children, the ups and downs in my life, and what my Agreement may have been—if it even exists.

I've never felt the urge to tell anyone, any more than I felt the need to tell someone my hair is brown — it just is.

Perhaps there are many out there that believe the same thing, perhaps there are just a few. Perhaps I'm the only one. It doesn't matter because it's a private thing, and it should be that way for everyone.

So, enjoy the quiet, personal concept of OneSelf, if you choose to believe in this possibility. If you choose not to, that's fine too, as it doesn't matter, and you can laugh at the absurdity.

I might even laugh with you.

OneSelf

Mark Bradford

# What Now?

Here it comes, right? This is the part where I summarize all this, and explain that if you think this was all interesting it's just the tip of the iceberg, right? You're pretty sure that now that you know this you can reach further enlightenment by taking my *Enlightenment In Only 30 Days* course or attend one of my *The OneSelf Divinity* seminars or subscribe to my daily OneSelf affirmations newsletter or subscribe through a pay service, etc.

Nope. There's no course, no webinar, or newsletter, no additional investment. I don't pass the collection plate, and I certainly don't request more of your money to tell you about a private connection you have with yourself.

Let that sentence sink in.

143

All you get is this book, which should have hopefully explained things in enough detail. To offer anything else would contradict what was just explained about this and would tarnish my impeccable luster as the messenger.

***OneSelf is a private thing, that if exists does so regardless of what I say or don't say about it.***

That's one of the beautiful things about it—it's immutable, or it doesn't exist. Neither of those things should affect how you go about your life.

# I certainly don't request more of your money to tell you about a private connection you have with yourself.

That cold you feel? It's the cool wind of personal responsibility, and I'm not handing you the Blanket Of Giving Up Responsibility—even if you want to throw money at me.

Don't.

I write the books as they present themselves to me, so if a sequel to this book presents itself I will do my best to relay it to you again.

Take care of yourself, do the right thing, and consider whether any of this is true. Enjoy it, incorporate it into your belief system, embrace it. At least give it some thought—it might help you hone your own concept of faith and what else is out there.

## I'm sorry

If you've read the book—actually *read* it and not an excerpt or just heard of it or just read a title and you are offended—then I apologize. My purpose was not to offend but instead to educate about this hypothetical possibility. If you have something to say about it know that I already said it to myself, so I am cheerfully saving you the effort and frustration in trying to set me straight.

I'm sorry if I spelled god with a capital letter inappropriately or not with a capital letter when called for. I tried to be consistent, and I don't ascribe to the "use a hyphen instead of the "o'" rule. It's a word and words are beautiful and we should not fear their use. The fear plunges us back into the dark ages. The avoidance of words—the ascribing of too much power to them—is what causes the problems, not solves them.

# Who are you?

I'm curious. Who exactly reads a book (in its entirety) about a new, hypothetical explanation for *all* spirituality? It certainly takes commitment, an open mind, and a desire to learn something new. If that describes you, then I'm honored that you spent your time and effort absorbing, considering and perhaps even agreeing. I don't just dismiss that.

Perhaps you read this because you thought it might be a fun thought experiment; if that's the case then that too takes all of the above. Even if your current belief system is unshakable (though I doubt that is the case[37]) you probably still have room for consideration. After all, it's faith we are talking about, not math.

# Who am I?

If the OneSelf exists regardless of your belief in it, and it is not an evangelical belief system, and is a separate thing entirely from our existence, then what's the point of writing a book about it? In fact, what's the point of reading one then? The next steps are missing, aren't they? After your "enlightenment" we would then move to the enrollment, then the dues, then the changing of the behavior. Then the enlistment of the cause, and then the evangelism. But we don't do that, because it's not part of OneSelf. You're off the hook.

---

[37] Because doubt is healthy.

So again, what's the point of writing a book about a word that doesn't need to be spread and changes nothing to be aware of?

Maybe that's my job?    Maybe that's my unique journey—to be the messenger.    Or maybe, far more likely, it is just another manifestation of my core talents—to perceive from an angle most others do not, and then build / create / disseminate / explain.

That's far more probable.  So that's who I am—the explainer—and this is just another thing I encountered that I want to explain for you.

As I have said there was no life changing event that created my belief in OneSelf.    However, I have lived a very "rich" life in which I have experienced and endured things that I would not wish on others —unless that of course is their journey.

I wrote—and rewrote—many times a section here on my experiences in an attempt to convey that not only have I had some pretty grueling experiences, but that I understand you if you've had them too.  It just never came outright, and this isn't a book about my hardships.

I can tell you that my understanding of the hypothetical concept that is OneSelf came about regardless of my experiences in life—good or bad. Remove all the suffering or add more, and I would have still thought this made sense.

## My tone

Tone is a very important thing. Comedies are funny, murder mysteries are serious, horrors are intense, personal development books are... well, boring. Non-fiction is dry, and religious publications are for the most part oppressive. I'm not referring to little quips and passages or even sermons; I'm talking about the actual instruction book that goes along with the religion (or in some cases spirituality). Even if you disagree with that you'll agree that they are very authoritative and absolute. They have to be—they are defining something that in itself *must* be absolute. Remember how we touched on the requirement that religion answer everything? If they don't then the omnipotent and omniscient deity is no longer either.

I could have written this book in a very authoritative, very biblical, very epic, very Silmarillion[38]-like manner. But...

Because I wrote this with the understanding from the very beginning that it is hypothetical, that it *is* faith—that it is by very definition unprovable—it gave me some leeway.

Because I have no desire to create a cult, to design an organized religion with buildings and dues and punishments, I don't have to be absolute.

---

[38] The Silmarillion by J.R.R. Tolkien. Have you read it? Oh my god. There's no way you actually made it through that book.

Because I could be completely wrong and that I respect each person's belief and that even if I'm right about all this, it really doesn't matter; it allows me to be less than authoritative.

Instead, I could be me, and deliver information in a way that wasn't threatening and in some cases was (and you may disagree strongly) amusing. I do not and did not in any way intend to be disrespectful. My intention is to describe to the best of my ability something that is hypothetical and intangible.

This book would have been a very different kind of publication had I delivered all of this in a strong, authoritative, serious, and absolute manner.

If anyone ever tries to deliver this same message about OneSelf in a way that is counter to how I presented it, then they are not talking about OneSelf.

They are talking about another organized religion.


## A curious revelation

As I said, it has been over 30 years since I came up with the concept of OneSelf. Even though I have carried it with me, reflected on it, etc., something curious happened recently.

It felt *different*.

I'm referring specifically to "prayer." I found that often I was not only thinking to my HighSelf about issues, stumbling blocks in my life, but also thinking that some all powerful being would sweep in and right the wrongs and solve all the injustices and make things better. In other words, I was praying in the standard fashion, in which one prays to an all powerful caretaker being—and those requests took the form of "give me something."

# Prayer turns into concrete actions instead of just waiting around for something to drop out of the sky.

Of course that never happened. I didn't receive that thing—in my humble opinion of course, and you may protest that statement—but I kept doing it. I kept praying to make it better, to deliver the item, the goal, the reward[39].

However, once I solidified my thoughts in the form of this book I thought a bit more about prayer, and pleas for help. Once I made a request or asked a question, I immediately thought, "So what can I do about it?" There was no emptiness of "putting it out to the universe." There was no "praying really hard

---

[39] I understand that you might suggest that this is what form prayer really should take anyway, and that I was "doing it wrong."

and waiting for a sign."

Since I knew, hypothetically, that whatever requests or questions or communication I was making was being done with a higher being *that only had control over me* that changed things.

The request ended, and I then thought about what *I could do* about it. If you want to meet a special person, you can commune and meditate and even talk at the ceiling, but when you're done you then think concrete, tangible thoughts about what you can do about it. You think that you should probably get out more, be more outgoing, join groups, and introduce yourself more. If you want success, then you think about what kind of success you want, what you're willing to do to obtain it, and why you actually want it. You define it a bit better than a general happy needful feeling.

Prayer turns into concrete actions instead of just waiting around for something to drop out of the sky.

I'm just saying that if you remove the concept entirely of a caretaker presence that has control over the environment things have a different feel to them.

I think it's the latter that turns off a lot of people on religion in general—the requests to the magic wish being and then the sitting back. It is why people go from prayer to saying "I sent it out to the Universe" even though that's essentially the same thing with just a better label.

I'm not suggesting that everyone who prays for
good fortune or changes prays and then just remains
blissfully ignorant of the environment, nor am I
saying they have no concept of cause and effect.
I'm just saying that if you remove the concept
entirely of a caretaker presence that has control over
the environment things have a different feel to
them.

*It's easy to sit there and say you'd
like to have more money. And I guess
that's what I like about it—it's easy.
Just sitting there, rocking back and
forth, wanting that money.*

*- Jack Handey*

You pray for a change, and then you think, "So
what does that mean? What can I do to affect that
change? Is there something I am doing that is
preventing that from happening?" So in a way you
pray to your HighSelf and then immediately talk to
your LowSelf—*you*.

It feels empowering. It feels like you have a heck
of a lot more control over your life. It helps you to
understand where your control ends. That in itself
can be very enlightening, and, even those who

strongly believe in traditional prayer, sing the praises of letting go of control of those things you cannot control.

This is one of the biggest lessons learned for those who have a lot of stress in their lives—they find out that they have far less control over things in their lives.

I was one of those people many years ago when I became a single, full-time father of two kids.

> This is one of the biggest lessons learned for those who have a lot of stress in their lives–they find out that they have far less control over things in their lives.

I would suggest that anyone who prays tries this form of prayer—the limited kind that is immediately followed by "What actions can I perform towards this goal?"

There is a distinct lack of victimhood in doing so. There is no longer a repeating pattern of *Woe is me and repeat.*

Even those that profess no religion or even spirituality benefit from and may already be doing this.

Think about it. It was an eye-opener for me.

# In closing

Perhaps this has given you a lot to think about; perhaps it's opened your mind to another possibility. Maybe this is a just a fun thought experiment and a work of complete fiction. Maybe that's what all religion and spirituality is?

If I have entertained you, then that is great. If I seem to have enlightened you, then that's wonderful.

As I say in the dedication "Believe it or not, it doesn't matter." That sentence is a gem because it has multiple meanings. Believe OneSelf or not, because *it doesn't matter to Oneself if you believe it or not*—it just is. And, believe it or not, *this concept doesn't matter, because you already made it this far in life* and and already have the tools to keep going.

Have faith in yourself first and foremost.

With Love,

- Mark Bradford

OneSelf

# $\mathcal{GLOSSARY}$

The following are concepts and terms discussed in this OneSelf book. They are listed here for completeness and to reduce any possible confusion.

Obviously this is a non-exhaustive list, as a list of that completeness would triple the size of this book. The terms listed are from the perspective of the hypothetical OneSelf belief, as that is the most helpful presentation of these terms in the scope of this book, and it is assumed that the reader already has a basic understanding of spirituality and religion. Your definitions may differ.

**LowSelf—** This is you, your current physical form.

**HighSelf—**The theoretical higher being that you are a part of. This being, for all intents and purposes, is also you. It exists in an expanded dimension and is a higher form of what you know life to be.

**OneSelf—**When the HighSelf and LowSelf are combined, they create the OneSelf. This is the complete being that is a combination of the higher form with all the memories, attributes, trials, and experiences of the LowSelf. The OneSelf splits into the HighSelf and LowSelf, so that the LowSelf can gather experiences on a journey and then recombine. This may happen only once or an infinite amount of times or any number in between, hypothetically.

**The Agreement—**When the OneSelf is ready to split, it agrees to pursue a certain journey. Part of the agreement is the circumstances in which the LowSelf is created. This can take the form of any situation, good or bad. It is difficult to understand that you would agree to a life of hardship, or a limited life—span, physically, mentally— that is what makes each journey unique.

**Theist—**A person that believes in the existence of god or gods. This is listed here not because it is used commonly (it is not used outside of religion and philosophical circles) but because it is the root word of many terms. You would be a *theist* if you believe in the hypothetical belief system that is

OneSelf. Sort of.

**Atheist**— A person who does not believe in the existence of god or gods, the opposite of a "theist." The "a" denotes "not" as in "atypical" is "not typical."

It does not matter to OneSelf whether you have belief or not because it exists or it does not and is not affected by belief. An awareness of OneSelf is just that—an awareness. And, lack thereof does not necessarily enhance the journey. For some it may detract from it.

**Monotheistic**—A belief that is based on the existence of *one* god, like most "modern" religions. "Mono" as in "one." If you regard your HighSelf as a god, then you would technically have a monotheistic belief, although some religious scholars may split hairs between this entity and that of a god.

**Polytheistic**—A belief that is based on more than one god. "Poly" as in "many." Is OneSelf monotheistic or polytheistic? It is polytheistic in that there are more than one of these entities—in fact one for each sentient being. However, since you only really have contact with your HighSelf it is essentially a closed system of just one deity.

One could also argue that the other HighSelves are affecting the other LowSelves and thus creating a polytheistic environment of flux.

**Religion**—(also known as "organized religion.") Religion is a set of rules and a belief system that is almost always written down with reference works. Most religions use parables and stories to demonstrate a point so that the lesson is not only easy to understand but appears to have already happened. Religions typically consist of a large group of believers and a hierarchal structure. Followers, laypersons, pastors/rabbis/clerics, etc. are part of this hierarchal structure.

There is no hierarchal structure in OneSelf, save for the two participants that create the third being—you, your HighSelf and the OneSelf.

**Spirituality**—To be "spiritual but not religious" is to believe in more than meets the eye, but not have assigned any particular religion rights over your belief. Those who profess to be spiritual are giving up far less control than those that belong to a religion. Absent from spirituality are gods and hierarchal structures. One does not seek out the leader of a spirituality except in the case that one might seek out a solemn guru who seems to have gotten in touch with the particular spirituality of interest, as they can learn from his teachings. But he does not seek them out to gather a following—in fact he typically is opposed to such things.

OneSelf could be considered a spirituality in that there is no guide book or set of rules, and the only deity involved, theoretically, is the HighSelf.

One could seek out a guru in that the guru might clarify things, or open their eyes to something they hadn't considered. But ultimately the path of those that believe in OneSelf is up to them.

And since it doesn't matter to OneSelf whether you believe in it or not, instructions aren't necessarily helpful.

**Church**—A church is typically expected to be a physical building. It is also used to represent a group, as in "the church of _____." OneSelf does not require a building, as the congregation numbers exactly one, and the OneSelf exists regardless of where you are or what you do.

**Congregation**—A group of people assembled for worship, typically in a church. The gathering space can take many forms but the key to a congregation is that the individuals *congregate*. Those who believe in the hypothetical existence of the OneSelf would not and do not congregate for the purpose of OneSelf. A congregation requires, ultimately, a leader of some kind. OneSelf does not have a leader, nor does it need, require, or accept anyone to be inserted between the LowSelf and the HighSelf.

**Pastor / Cleric**—The leader of an organized religion. The person that wrote this book is not a pastor nor is he a cleric. He is not the leader of the OneSelf religion because it is not a religion and requires no earthly representation. It is or it is not, and nothing anyone does affects that.

**Ritual**—A series of actions performed regularly and invariably. By performing a ritual, a person can and does affect certain brain patterns. Rituals exist to set a tone, as the actions act as a flag or indicator for a mood. performing a ritual can create a solemn moment (as in the case of a candle light vigil), create a feeling of gratitude (as in the case of prayer before a meal), or seriousness (as in standing at attention).

Sitting and breathing deeply in meditation is also a ritual.

Rituals are not necessarily only religious in nature and are used in all areas that require an affirmation of changing in mood—family, business, ceremonies, etc. They are a part of our lives, our civilization, and our culture.

OneSelf does not contain any rituals, other than perhaps meditating to clear one's mind in an effort to find one's path (or at least let go of noise). In this it is no different than many spiritualities (including yoga).

Not even this is required, as OneSelf does not require an awareness.

Mark Bradford

OneSelf

# *ABOUT THE AUTHOR*

Mark Bradford produces and hosts a weekly podcast about Time, Energy and Resources that also features interviews with amazing people. Listen to *The Alchemy for Life* podcast for more insight, on iTunes and most other podcast providers. Subscribe and you won't miss them.

www.alchemyfor.life

Mark produces *The Status Game* series of books and card game that helps demonstrate, educate, and enlighten people about an invisible but very real aspect on how we connect and what we like.

His answers have over two million answer views on
Quora—a question and answer community.
Follow Mark on Instagram for announcements and
things related to his content—books, podcasts, etc.

# @authormarkbradford

It's a fun feed with daily posts.  Have a question?
Ask it on the podcast.

To hire Mark to speak at your event, or engage him
as a coach contact him at:

# media@alchemyfor.life

## Books by Mark Bradford

# Nonfiction:

### *The Status Game*
Navigating the perilous waters of dating and online dating.
With a sense of humor.

### *The Status Game II*
How status is the key to all relationships—business and
personal.

### *OneSelf*
Faith of a simpler, more direct kind. Or just nonsense.

### *Alchemy for Life*
Everything you need to know about Life Coaching in one
book. And 16 formulas for success.

### *The Status Game III: Discover Your Gages*
The complete Status Game compendium including workbook
companion to *The Status Game & The Status Game II*

### *Three Voices*
*The three Voices you use to communicate with yourself and
others.*

# Fiction:

### *The Sword and the Sunflower*
The epic, coming-of-age hero's journey set in a far future.

### *Amira*
Book two of The Sword and the Sunflower.

### *Upside Down*
The 1,000 year history of the saints. The prequel to *The
Sword and the Sunflower* duet.

OneSelf

Mark Bradford

www.ingramcontent.com/pod-product-compliance
Lightning Source LLC
Chambersburg PA
CBHW071533040426
42452CB00008B/992

*9 7 8 1 7 3 3 6 6 2 2 0 8*